W9-BGS-310

9-7-2

Rubens *Drawings and Sketches*

NC 266 .R8 R63 1977
Rubens, Peter Paul, 1577-
1640.
Rubens

WITHDRAWN

Rubens
Drawings and Sketches

Catalogue of an exhibition at
the Department of Prints and Drawings
in the British Museum, 1977

by John Rowlands

RITTER LIBRARY
BALDWIN-WALLACE COLLEGE

Published for the Trustees of the British Museum
by British Museum Publications Limited

Cover: Detail from the *Martyrdom of St Paul*
(cat. no.190)

Frontispiece: Design for the title-page to the
works of Ludovicus Blosius, 1632
(cat. no.221)

© 1977 The Trustees of the British Museum
Reprinted 1978

ISBN 0 7141 0753 0 cased
ISBN 0 7141 0754 9 paper

Published by British Museum Publications
Ltd, 6 Bedford Square, London WC1B 3RA

Designed by James Shurmer

Set in Monophoto Bembo

Printed in Great Britain by Balding and
Mansell Ltd, London and Wisbech

British Library Cataloguing in Publication Data

Rowlands, John
    Rubens: drawings and sketches.
    1. Rubens, *Sir* Peter Paul
    2. British Museum
    3. Drawings, Flemish – Exhibitions
    I. British Museum
      741.9'493   NC266.R8

Contents

Acknowledgements

The Trustees wish to express their thanks to Her Majesty the Queen for graciously consenting to lend three important drawings from the Royal Collection at Windsor; also to the Trustees of the National Gallery and the National Gallery of Scotland, of the Metropolitan Museum and the Pierpont Morgan Library in New York, of the Museum of Fine Arts in Boston and of the National Gallery of Art in Washington; the Director of the Victoria and Albert Museum; the Visitors of the Ashmolean Museum, Oxford; the Governors of Dulwich College; the British Library Board; the Chairman and Committee of the City Museum and Art Gallery, Plymouth; the Sterling and Francine Clark Institute at Williamstown; and the Director of the Fogg Museum of Harvard University. They are also grateful to the Trustees of the Chatsworth Settlement and to those private collectors whose generosity has so greatly contributed to the exhibition: Mrs Humphrey Brand, the Marquess of Cholmondeley, Mrs Eliot Hodgkin, Count Antoine Seilern, the late Duke of Portland, Lady Anne Bentinck and others who wish to remain anonymous.

Thanks are also due for help of various kinds to Mr Jacob Bean, Mr and Mrs Hans Calmann, Miss Shaunagh Fitzgerald, Mr David Freedberg, Professor Julius Held, Dr Anne-Marie Logan, the Hon. Mrs Roberts, Mr Anthony Radcliffe, Mr Andrew Robison, Miss Eleanor Sayre, Miss Felice Stampfle, Mr Edward Speelman, Mr Julien Stock and Mr T. S. Wragg. Thanks are also due to those colleagues in other Departments of the British Museum who have so kindly assisted in the preparation of the Exhibition.

Mr John Rowlands, Deputy Keeper in the Department, has been responsible for organising the exhibition and writing the catalogue. He has received much assistance of various kinds from Mrs Ilse O'Dell-Franke and Mrs Rosi Schilling, to whom we would like to express our grateful thanks. Valuable assistance in the preparation and checking of the catalogue has been given by Mr Martin Royalton-Kisch, Research Assistant in the Department, who has also written many of the introductory notes to the various sections of the catalogue.

J. A. Gere

Introduction

When all around us today we hear the dire predictions of the prophets of gloom it is providential that 1977 brings with it the celebration of Rubens's genius on the occasion of the four hundredth anniversary of the artist's birth. For of all the great masters of European art none can outdo him in his direct expression of a zest for life. His art is itself principally an exuberant celebration of the good things of this world. This is not of course a complete picture of his artistic personality, but it is true that vitality is his abiding characteristic. In his work the dominant mood is one of measured optimism. The same can be said of his life. For under the influence of his brother's teacher, Lipsius, Rubens as an urbane Catholic gentleman-artist was attracted by the moderation of stoicism. But from his correspondence we can see that when tragedy struck his honest nature disclosed him as a man of feeling.

Despite his manifest and almost universally acclaimed greatness it has to be admitted that many have found his art difficult to approach. Even among Rubens enthusiasts one often detects more admiration than love. In general it would be fair to say that many art lovers, including those who have no pretensions to more than a certain amount of general knowledge about art, and perhaps a little art history, tend to find Rubens's paintings somewhat forbidding. There is certainly some justification for this hesitancy because to enjoy the full rich flavour of Rubens it is necessary to take trouble to gain some background information about the circumstances under which Rubens worked, which are quite foreign to us now. Rubens was by temperament and in practice an intellectual artist, but not in any austere or dry sense. At every turn his cultured and civilised mind is at work and it can be an exciting experience for scholars and non-specialists alike to delve into the often quite complex, certainly always fascinating, methods he adopted in the creation of his paintings.

Fortunately the key to an understanding of these processes is to be found in the subject of the 1977 exhibition, Rubens's drawings and oil-sketches. These works of his, because of the spontaneity of their execution, are more immediately appealing to us than the finished paintings. As such they will no doubt be much more readily acceptable to those who not only want a pleasurable introduction to Rubens, but would also like to begin to see how his mind works. The basis of the current exhibition has been the British Museum's rich collection of drawings supplemented by a choice collection of drawings and oil-sketches from public and private collections in this country, Switzerland and the United States. This occasion has made it necessary to examine afresh the Museum's collection of drawings attributed to Rubens. It may come as a surprise that many drawings which have been thought in the past to be by Rubens are now considered to be of questionable authenticity.

Unfortunately the question of the status of many drawings attributed to him has been a continuing bone of contention amongst specialists for many years. Such matters of attribution with Rubens have provoked almost more disagreement among scholars than is the case with nearly any other master one can think of, possibly even including Rembrandt. Although many of the drawings have an inscription on them in an early hand *Rubens*, frequently spelt with two 'b's, none of his drawings has an authentic signature. One category of his drawings however, the book illustrations, and in particular the title-page designs (nos. 204–22), can usually be established with confidence as most of them can be connected with documented payments made by the publisher to the artist. But even here one can encounter problems. For instance, the somewhat faded condition of the *Christ crucified with the two thieves* (no. 208) seems to have persuaded Arthur M. Hind, Keeper of the Department of Prints and Drawings in the 1930s, to classify it as a School drawing in his catalogue of the Flemish seventeenth-century drawings in the Print Room which appeared in 1923. In making a systematic examination of those drawings kept in the Museum under Rubens's name we have often found ourselves at variance with Hind's assessment of their status as noted in his 1923 catalogue. In fairness to Hind, however, it must be said that he compiled his catalogue under the considerable disadvantage of being an early worker in the field, in fact, before the modern upsurge in the serious study of Rubens by scholars had begun in earnest. This new critical spirit was heralded by Glück and Haberditzl's notable anthology published in 1928, which consists of a corpus of 241 drawings. This publication was much less complete than its authors imagined but constituted a major step forward over previous efforts at an understanding of Rubens's draughtsmanship.

Coming fresh to Rubens studies from another field, I have found the vetting of the drawings a fascinating voyage of discovery, even though the work has meant that a sizeable number of them have had to be down-graded. It may be interesting for readers to learn of some examples of these rejected drawings, particularly as for the most part problematical drawings have not been included in the exhibition, as it has been thought desirable that the visitor's view of Rubens's draughtsmanship should not be unnecessarily blurred with difficult or dubious cases.

An interesting example is the *Portrait of Hélène Fourment* (Hind 96, fig. 1) which Hind described as a preparatory drawing by Rubens for his portrait of his second wife, formerly in the collection of the Baron Alphonse de Rothschild. It has something of the pretty superficiality which is more commonly found in the eighteenth century than in the seventeenth century. The lack of structure about the sitter's features is not to be explained away merely because of the drawing's sketchiness. Similarly we do not find elsewhere in any of Rubens's drawings such a meaningless rendering of the hair. Nothing is known of the drawing's history before the end of the eighteenth century; however, this ignorance is not in any case conclusive either for or against the drawing's status. If a drawing has a distinguished pedigree it might prejudice us in its favour, but it does of course do no more than indicate that a series of notable collectors could have admired its qualities. One cannot really do better than compare this portrait with that of the second wife in the collection of Count Antoine Seilern (no. 155) for a swift appreciation of the deficiencies of the Museum's portrait.

Because of the considerable sway that Rubens held over later generations of artists, especially those in eighteenth-century France, there has been a tendency for the works of such artists to be tinged with a flavour of Rubens that has caused them to be mistaken later by collectors as authentic Rubens. A single example will suffice though there are more in the Museum's collection. The study of an old man looking up (Hind 102, fig. 2) so strongly reflects the romantic sentiment of the middle and later years of the eighteenth century that it is inconceivable that this could even belong to the same century as Rubens, let alone be by him.

The most important reason for the clouding of opinion about the status of Rubens's drawings is his practice of working as the head of a large and highly organised studio. Very many of his paintings were produced to a greater or lesser degree by assistants, and only in the final stages would Rubens pull the work together with deft strokes at strategic points on the canvas. The nature of his drawings and hence their characteristics were affected by their use in the studio, for Rubens adopted strikingly different modes of expression according to the purpose for which the drawing was intended. Rubens was employing his assistants to produce drawings after his paintings as designs for reproductive engravings to advertise his

work. Almost without exception these drawings were done in this way and were usually executed in black chalk. Rubens would then work up the design in bodycolour, frequently adjusting details to suit the translation of the design to the engraved medium. An excellent example of this sort of design is his *Flight into Egypt* (no. 171). In this drawing we can clearly see what has been done by the assistant and what is by Rubens, as the work in bodycolour is so superior in quality to the initial sketch. In many of these drawings he has so thoroughly reworked the design that one can no longer make out the assistant's contribution. A good example of such an initial drawing, but executed by Rubens, not an assistant, is that for *Obsidio Bredana,* a book about the famous siege of Breda. Although this has been quite obscured from view by the reworking in bodycolour, it was fortunately discovered when the drawing was recently lifted from its mount that it was possible to see Rubens's initial drawing visible through the paper. Visitors will be able to gain an impression of this initial sketch from a photograph in which the design has been reversed so that it appears in the same direction as it would have done on the sheet.

Many drawings were the inevitable products of Rubens's busy studio, for he had neither the time nor the energy to produce himself literal copies after his own compositions. Perhaps it is worth recalling Otto Sperling's famous account of a visit to Rubens's studio in 1621. He tells us that he came upon Rubens painting in his studio, having Tacitus read to him, while at the same time he was also dictating a letter. Sperling says that Rubens began to talk to him, answering his questions while continuing to work. Sperling's impression was that Rubens was showing off. It is possible that Rubens was staging a special performance, but it does seem most likely that for Rubens such methods of work could not have been so very extraordinary. With all his commitments he was continually under pressure and could only get by through good organisation and delegating as much as he possibly could to his assistants. Sometimes the work on a painting would be so far devolved that responsibility for the design was given to another artist who himself produced his own drawing. A notable example of such a commission is the *Prometheus Bound* at Philadelphia of about 1612–18. As testimony of Snyders's collaboration in this painting we have his pen drawing for the *Eagle* (no.80) which is modelled on Michelangelo, probably at Rubens's suggestion.

In many ways the most interesting drawings by Rubens are his preliminary sketches for his commissions. For in these he reveals his creative powers and vigour at its most intense. They could be either on paper or on panel. As far as we can tell he did not work according to any strict method. For example he did not always put his preliminary ideas first on paper. Sometimes he may well have started to work at once on panel, and to produce his first free sketch on that. Naturally enough he was governed by the convenience of the moment.

The majority of Rubens's preliminary studies reveal their purpose to us at once as they are so obviously the result of trial and error. On such sheets Rubens is continually making alterations, working towards his solution until the result is a maze of lines. No more magnificent example can be provided than the sheet covered with studies of Hercules undertaking some of his various labours (no.184 *recto*). Here we have Rubens in full spate pouring out his thoughts onto paper. Such spontaneity and accomplished alterations leave no room for doubt that we have before us the work of the master himself. For these are not the fumblings of an unpractised student but the inspired stirrings of genius. This freedom of expression in his draughtsmanship, unusual in a northern artist since the days of Dürer, was something that Rubens had evidently absorbed during his years in Italy. In this searching out on paper Rubens is seeking through trial and error to uncover an ideally satisfying solution. Rubens's fertile invention is particularly well illustrated by his sheet with studies of a couple dancing (no.178 *verso*). Such spontaneous calligraphy should in my view form the basis for our judging the quality of drawings attributed to Rubens, providing, of course, that we do not thereby exclude the produce of more finished and studied moments. The art of making a transition from his freely expressed drawings to his more finished designs is that we do not lower our standards of excellence but make allowances for the fact that differences of function must inevitably call for differences of expression. The art of judging Rubens's drawings clearly is that we have always to appreciate the important role that Rubens's assistants played in the process of creating his paintings, and that the work of his assistants will be mistaken for that of the master's if the function of a particular drawing is not understood aright. For hardly any drawings exist that have been drawn for their own sake and have not some immediate or potential utility.

Very few of Rubens's initial rough compositional sketches in which the barest outlines of the composition have been drafted have survived. The reason for this is obvious enough. This was because such thoughts were at once superseded by a clearer, more fully worked out realisation. One or two of these studio 'cast-offs' have been rescued from oblivion. Fortunately, although the British Museum has none of these great rarities, it has been possible to borrow for the exhibition a slight but nonetheless fascinating sketch done in red chalk for the altar piece *The Last Communion of St Francis* (no. 84 *recto*). Neither in this sketch nor in another similar drawing in pen of the lower part of the composition now at Antwerp has the central act of the composition been determined. For only in the painting itself is the priest holding up the Host before St Francis, whereas in both sketches the priest is represented as being on the point of offering the Host to the saint. This important change made possible the upward gaze of St Francis which constitutes the dramatic focal point of the whole composition in the final painting. The determination of this pictorial key which gives a significance to the painting would no doubt have been arrived at when Rubens painted his oil-sketch, which was the next stage in the process before he produced the large painting itself. On this the basic arrangement of the whole work was usually finally fixed, although there are instances where Rubens continued experimenting with ideas on the panel.

With Rubens demarcation between painting and drawing was never clearly defined. The oil-sketch was at times a brush drawing in brown which happened to be on panel with often only some figures slightly coloured. Several very exciting panels have come down to us on which Rubens has worked so intensely that it is difficult for us now to unravel their complexities. A more straight-forward but no less stirring example is the *Lion Hunt* from the National Gallery (no. 88), in which we see Rubens initially trying out the central action of the composition in the upper right-hand corner of the sketch, before proceeding to work out his elaboration of the whole composition on the main part of the panel.

The class of drawing in which Rubens's genius as a draughtsman shines out with particular splendour is his chalk drawings from the life model. Rubens for the most part did these after he had executed and gained the client's approval of a coloured oil-sketch for the proposed painting. At this stage, as it were, each of the actors in Rubens's baroque drama had been given his or her allotted place in the whole scheme. They are executed for the most part in black chalk on rough paper with an extraordinary sureness of hand. The contrast between these drawings and the intricate jumble of his preliminary 'try outs' could hardly be more stark. This lucidity of course was a necessity, as these drawings were an essential guide for Rubens's assistants, and it is no accident that the majority of such drawings date from the time when the demand on Rubens's studio was at its most intense. With these clear images, uncluttered with superfluous lines, his skilled assistants could work with precision, knowing what was required of them. The establishing of an intelligible chronology for Rubens's drawings is frequently very difficult, as none has been dated by the artist. It is furthermore not sufficient for us just to connect a particular drawing with a particular commission in order to be able to say that this drawing was done specifically for it. There are many instances of drawings being used over a period of years in successive commissions. This capacity of Rubens for using repeatedly the same models in new guises is one of the important factors of his work. His genius for stage-managing not only elements from earlier compositions but also those drawn from heterogeneous sources gives the study of Rubens's creative processes its own special brand of intellectual satisfaction. By some strange wizardry most of these visual quotations from the works of others are so subtly done that when we do become aware of them we are at once struck by Rubens's extraordinary power of so thoroughly assimilating these sources that he makes them part of his own individual vocabulary.

John Rowlands

Chronology

1577 Peter Paul Rubens is born on 28 June at Siegen, Westphalia. His parents came from Antwerp.

1578 Rubens's family settles in Cologne.

1587 Rubens's father dies, after which Rubens's mother returns with her family to Antwerp.

1589 Rubens attends the school of Romandus Verdonck.

1590 Rubens enters the service of Countess Marguerite de Ligne-d'Arenberg.

1591 He begins to paint and starts his training in the studio of Tobias Verhaecht, the landscape painter.

1592 He may have studied for a time under Adam van Noort.

1596 Rubens probably entered Otto van Veen's studio, a painter much influenced by late Italian Mannerism.

1598 Rubens becomes a member of the Antwerp guild of St Luke.

1600 On 9 May Rubens leaves for Italy. He enters the service of the Duke of Mantua, Vincenzo Gonzaga, as court painter, probably through the influence of the Archduke Albert, Regent of the Netherlands. On 5 October he is present at the marriage by proxy of Marie de Médicis to Henry IV of France in Florence.

1601 He arrives in Rome in July and stays there until April 1602. He is commissioned by the Archduke Albert to paint a triptych for Santa Croce in Gerusalemme, Rome.

1603 The Duke of Mantua sends Rubens on a diplomatic mission escorting some presents for Philip III of Spain and his chief minister, the Duke of Lerma. He travels via Florence, Pisa and Alicante, reaching the Spanish court at Valladolid on 13 May. He paints the series of *Apostles*, and the equestrian portrait of the Duke of Lerma, now in the Prado, Madrid.

1604 Back in Mantua, Rubens is granted an annual pension of 400 ducats by the Duke.

1605 Rubens is commissioned by the Duke to paint the *Trinity adored by Vincenzo Gonzaga and his Family* (Mantua); the *Transfiguration* (Nancy); the *Baptism of Christ* (Antwerp).

1606 Rubens visits Genoa where he paints the signed *Portrait of Brigida Spinola* (Bankes collection, Kingston Lacy). Rubens stays for the last time in Rome, where he has contact with Adam Elsheimer and Paul Brill. He buys Caravaggio's *Virgin mourned by the Apostles*

(Louvre). He is commissioned to paint the high altar for the Chiesa Nuova with the *Virgin adored by Saints*, the first version of which was refused (now in the Grenoble Museum); the second version finished in October 1609 is still *in situ*.

1608   Rubens's mother is critically ill and he leaves for Antwerp in October; however, his mother dies in November before the arrival of her son.

1609   Rubens, through the influence of Nicolas Rockox, the alderman, gains the important commission of the *Adoration of the Magi* (Prado) for the Town Hall, Antwerp. He marries Isabella Brant, and paints the double portrait of himself and his bride, now in Munich. He is appointed court painter to the Archduke Albert and the Infanta Isabella.

1611   Rubens purchases a new home on 4 January, a sixteenth-century house which he adapts for his convenience. His daughter Clara Serena is born. He is besieged with innumerable applications from young men wishing to become his apprentices. He completes the painting of the *Raising of the Cross* (Antwerp Cathedral) and begins to paint the *Descent from the Cross*.

1612   He travels to Spa, where he paints the portrait of the *Earl of Arundel* (now lost). He becomes a designer to the Plantin Press, now managed by his childhood friend, Balthasar Moretus.

1613   He paints the signed and dated *Jupiter and Callisto* (Kassel) and for Moretus illustrates the *Opticorum* of Franciscus Aquilonius.

1614   His first son Albert is born. On 28 April his triptych of the *Descent from the Cross* is installed in Antwerp Cathedral. He executes the signed and dated *Susanna and the Elders* (Stockholm), *Venus frigida* (Antwerp) and the *Pietà* (Vienna).

1615   He paints for Nicholas Rockox the *Incredulity of St Thomas* (Antwerp). He secures the collaboration of the landscape painter, Lucas van Uden, and the engraver, Pieter Soutman.

1616   He paints the *Last Judgement* (Munich) for the Jesuit church at Neuburg.

1617   *Lamentation over the dead Christ* (Antwerp) is ordered for the tomb of the merchant, Jan Michielsen.

1618   Work is completed on the extension to Rubens's town house in Antwerp. Nicolas, his second son, is born. Rubens acquires from Sir Dudley Carleton, British Ambassador at the Hague, a collection of antique marbles in exchange for ten paintings by him.

1619   The *Last Communion of St Francis* (Antwerp) is painted for the Church of the Recollects, Antwerp. Rubens is commissioned by Duke Wolfgang-Wilhelm of Bavaria to paint an *Adoration of the Shepherds* and the *Descent of the Holy Ghost* (Munich) for the Jesuit Church at Neuburg. He is given the copyright for his prints in France.

1620 *Christ on the Cross* 'Le coup de lance', (Antwerp), is painted for the Church of the Recollects. He paints the *'Small' Last Judgement*. He obtains the copyright for his prints in Holland. Rubens is commissioned on 29 March to design the ceiling paintings for the Church of St Carlo Borromeo, Antwerp. Van Dyck and Lucas Vorsterman begin to work for Rubens.

1621 He executes the *Fall of the Damned* (Munich), probably also painted for the Jesuit Church at Neuburg. Marie de Médicis approaches him to do an ambitious decorative scheme for the Palais de Luxembourg. Hans van Mildert, the sculptor, begins his collaboration with Rubens.

1622 In Paris in January he discusses the programme for the cycle with Marie de Médicis and signs a contract. He undertakes for Louis XIII the designs for a series of twelve tapestries of the *History of Constantine*. He quarrels and breaks with Vorsterman. Rubens publishes his *I Palazzi di Genova*, edited by Jacques Meursius.

1623 Rubens returns to Paris with nine uncompleted canvases for the Palais de Luxembourg. He begins his activity as a diplomat. His eldest daughter, Clara Serena, dies.

1624 The *Adoration of the Magi* (Antwerp) is painted for the Abbey Church of St Michael, Antwerp. Paul Pontius begins his collaboration with Rubens which continues until 1631.

1625 Rubens makes his third visit to Paris during which he delivers the remaining paintings for the Médicis cycle. Rubens is present at the marriage of Charles I to Henrietta Maria. On 12 June he is once more back in Antwerp, where he is visited by the Infanta Isabella. From August to February 1626 he is in Brussels but goes to Dunkirk in September 1625. He makes a brief visit to the German frontier to meet Wolfgang-Wilhelm of Bavaria. The Duke of Buckingham visits Rubens's town house in Antwerp in November.

1626 Isabella Brant dies on 20 June. He finishes the *Assumption* for the high altar of Antwerp Cathedral. He goes to Calais in December with works bought by the Duke of Buckingham.

1627 Rubens makes his fourth visit to Paris where he stays with the Baron de Vicq. In February he returns to Antwerp with the painter and diplomat Balthazar Gerbier. He visits Holland in July. He produces sketches and *modelli* for the series of seventeen tapestries commissioned for the Carmelite nuns at Madrid.

1628 Rubens leaves Antwerp on 28 or 29 August for Madrid, where he is on friendly terms with Velasquez, then twenty-nine years old.

1629 He arrives in Brussels from Spain on 13 May and embarks on 18 May at Dunkirk for London where he arrives on 5 June. He is received immediately in audience by Charles I at Greenwich on the following day.

1630 Rubens, on 3 March, takes his leave of Charles I who commissions him to paint the ceiling decoration of the banqueting hall of Whitehall Palace (still *in situ*). Rubens is again in Antwerp in April. He is commissioned to paint the altarpiece of St Ildefonso (Vienna).

On 9 December he marries Hélène Fourment, the 16-year-old daughter of Daniel Fourment, a rich tapestry dealer. Boetius à Bolswert, the engraver, begins working for Rubens.

1631 As a representative of the Infanta he is received by Marie de Médicis in September. At the end of December he is involved in negotiations with Frederick Henry, Prince of Orange.

1632 On 18 January Clara Johanna, the first child of Rubens and Hélène Fourment, is born. Rubens offers his resignation as the representative of the Infanta on 9 April. He starts his association with Christoffel Jegher, the wood-engraver.

1633 Frans Rubens is born on 12 July.

1634 He tries to free himself from his diplomatic responsibilities.

1635 On 17 April the Cardinal-Infante Ferdinand makes his triumphal entry into Antwerp. Rubens is made responsible for the decoration by the City Fathers and the whole scheme executed by a large team of artists under his supervision. Isabella Helena is born on 3 May. He buys the Château de Steen, near Malines, on 12 May.

1636 He is appointed court painter to the Cardinal-Infante Ferdinand. He begins work on the decorations for the Torre de la Parada, a royal hunting lodge near Madrid. He completes his work on the Whitehall ceiling.

1637 His son Peter Paul is born on 1 March. He paints the *Portrait of Hélène Fourment with her son, Frans and daughter, Clara Johanna* (Louvre). Jordaens and others assist with the execution of the Torre de la Parada decorations after Rubens's sketches.

1638 On 11 March the Torre de la Parada paintings are dispatched to Madrid. Rubens paints the portrait of *Hélène Fourment in a Fur Cloak* (Vienna) and the *Three Graces* (Madrid). Lucas Vorsterman works for Rubens again.

1639 Rubens is seriously ill. He makes his will on 16 December. Jordaens and others complete work in course of preparation in Rubens's studio.

1640 Rubens dies on 30 May at Antwerp and is buried in the Church of St Jacques.

1641 A daughter, Constance Albertine, is born posthumously.

1642 The sale of many of his paintings takes place on 17 March. A number are bought by the King of Spain's representative and include the *Peasant Dance,* the *Garden of Love,* and many other paintings now in the Prado Museum at Madrid.

List of works referred to in abbreviated form

Bartsch   Adam Bartsch, *Le Peintre Graveur* (21 vols). Vienna, 1803–21.

BMQ   *British Museum Quarterly*. London, from 1926–73.

Burchard-d'Hulst   L. Burchard and R. A.-d'Hulst, *Rubens Drawings* (2 vols). Brussels, 1963.

Burlington Magazine   *The Burlington Magazine*. London, from 1902.

Glück-Haberditzl   *Die Handzeichnungen von Peter Paul Rubens*, edited by G. Glück and F. M. Haberditzl. Berlin, 1928.

Held   J. S. Held, *Rubens – Selected Drawings* (2 vols). London, 1959.

Hind   Arthur M. Hind, *Catalogue of Drawings by Dutch and Flemish Artists preserved in the Department of Prints and Drawings in the British Museum*, vol. 2. London, 1923.

KdK   R. Oldenbourg, P. P. Rubens. *Des Meisters Gemälde Klassiker der Kunst*, vol. 5. Stuttgart-Berlin-Leipzig, 1921.

Magurn   *The Letters of Peter Paul Rubens*, translated and edited by R. S. Magurn. Cambridge, Mass., 1955.

MD   *Master Drawings*. New York, from 1963.

OMD   *Old Master Drawings*. London, 1926–40.

Puyvelde, *Esquisses*   L. van Puyvelde, *Les Esquisses de Rubens*, 2nd ed. Basle, 1948.

Rooses   M. Rooses, *L'oeuvre de P. P. Rubens, histoire et description de ses tableaux et dessins* (5 vols). Antwerp, 1886–92.

Schneevoogt   C. G. Voorhelm Schneevoogt, *Catalogue des Estampes Gravées d'après P. P. Rubens . . . .* Haarlem, 1873.

Smith   John Smith, *Catalogue Raisonné of the Works of the most eminent Dutch and Flemish Painters. Part the Second, containing the Life and Works of Peter Paul Rubens*. London, 1830.

van den Wijngaert   F. van den Wijngaert, *Inventaris der Rubeniaansche Prentkunst*. Antwerp, 1940.

van der Gucht   Gerard van der Gucht, *Antique Greek and Roman Coins, Gems etc. Engraved from original Drawings of Rubens*. London, 1740.

Wildenstein, 1950   Wildenstein & Co. Ltd., *Peter Paul Rubens*. London, 1950.

Wurzbach   A. von Wurzbach, *Niederländisches Künstler-Lexikon* (2 vols). Vienna and Leipzig, 1906 and 1910.

Catalogue

The Italian Period

Rubens was only twenty-two years old when he left Antwerp for Italy in May 1600. To judge from his earliest surviving drawings he was still an immature if highly promising artist. After eight years he returned to Antwerp with a mature baroque style, combining the artistic traditions of Italy and Flanders, that was the basis of his future reputation. Many of the drawings of this most crucial period in Rubens's development give us a close insight into his avid assimilation of renaissance, mannerist and antique art. He seems always to have kept a sketchbook to hand, constantly noting down impressions of anything that captured his imagination, whether works of art or women in national costume. At the same time he tackled his first known commissions and attempted the most complex dramatic scenes (e.g. nos. 16 and 21 in particular) as well as portraits (nos. 9, 10, 12, 29) and traditional religious subjects (e.g. *The Last Supper,* nos. 24–5). He experimented with every medium, but pen and ink, with their swift clarity, became the favourite both for sketching works of art and wrestling with his own ideas. For more carefully modelled studies a laborious process of cross-hatching in pen and ink (as in no. 21) was gradually abandoned in favour of wash or red or black chalk, handled with smooth precision (e.g. no. 14).

As a group the drawings of the Italian Period reveal Rubens's determination to master every medium and every kind of composition, and his readiness to absorb the lessons of the great masters of the past, while at the same time stretching his own technical and imaginative abilities to the full.

1a

1b

1a. Landsknechts fighting around a table
Pen and brown ink and wash. 13.2 × 17.4 cm
Provenance: P. J. Mariette.

1b. Scene in an inn
Pen and brown ink and brown and grey washes.
13.2 × 17.4 cm
Provenance: P. J. Mariette.
Switzerland, Private Collection

These two drawings on the same Mariette mount are copies made at the commencement of the artist's career. Despite Mariette's inscription indicating the contrary, they are after woodcuts by Hans Weiditz, not Hans Burgkmair, in the first book of Petrarch, *Von der Artzney bayder Glück . . .* (a German translation of *de Remediis utriusque fortunae*), Augsburg, H. Steyner, 1532. Four other copies by Rubens after Weiditz, similarly mounted, formerly in the Mariette Collection, are in the Louvre (Lugt, cat. nos. 1111–4). Two further drawings of the same type are in Rotterdam, and a third is in the Bonnat Collection in Bayonne.

2

3

The 'Costume Book'

This album of drawings consists mainly of costume studies copied from a compilation of material brought together by Antoine de Succa, most probably for a projected history of Flanders. Other sketches are copies after monuments, paintings and tapestries, prints by German masters, drawings done by European travellers in the Near East, and Persian miniature paintings. It is most likely that Rubens's purpose in copying these sources was to furnish himself with reference material for use in the studio. According to an eighteenth-century inscription on the fly-leaf, the volume consisted of 39 sheets, but at the Crozat sale of 1751 the volume was said to have 43 sheets. When it was acquired by the Museum in 1841, it consisted of 39 sheets, and one sheet, folio 6, was acquired later in the nineteenth century. Two further sheets (nos.9 and 10), formerly in the collection of Friedrich August II, King of Saxony (1797–1854), were acquired in 1949. A half sheet now in the Metropolitan Museum, New York, with Carolus, son of Ludovicus Simplex, and Gerberga, could also have come from the book. The same may be true of a drawing, a half sheet with Henry of Luxembourg and a nobleman, formerly in the collection of Ludwig Burchard.

Opinions differ about the dating of the contents of the book. J. S. Held has proposed that the drawings would fit best stylistically between 1610 and 1615. He states that Rubens could only have known the de Succa material after his return from Italy to Antwerp, and suggests very plausibly that these sketches should be linked with his appointment as court painter to the Archduke Albert and the Infanta Isabella in September 1609. Burchard-d'Hulst,

however, placed them before the journey to Italy in 1600. It would appear to be rather difficult to reconcile these views, but it does seem certain that the contents were drawn over a number of years. While the copies after the de Succa manuscript cannot have been done before 1609, nothing would have prevented Rubens from drawing earlier the copies after Burgkmair, Weiditz, and others. The costume studies of Castilian women are also likely to have been drawn when he was in Spain in 1603. Indeed it is quite possible that a major part of the album's contents not deriving from the de Succa manuscript was done prior to 1609.

Provenance: R. de Piles; P. Crozat.

1841-12-11-8 (1–39) and one page, folio 6 added later

Literature: M. J. Mariette, *Description . . . du Cabinet du feu M. Crozat,* 1741, p.97, no.845; G. F. Waagen, *Treasures of Art in Great Britain . . .,* i, 1854, pp.237–9; Hind, 119 (1–40); Held, under 163; Burchard-d'Hulst, under 1.

Drawings from the Costume Book

2. A knight on horseback and various other studies of horses, knights and armour

Pen and brown ink. 23.2 × 33.4 cm

1841-12-11-8 (21)

Literature: Hind, 119 (22).

The knight on the left is copied from Hans Burgkmair's woodcut of *St George* (no.3) and the horse's head on the right is from the same artist's woodcut of the *Emperor Maximilian in armour on horseback.*

Hans Burgkmair I (1473–1531)
3. St George

Chiaroscuro woodcut, with the tone-block printed in dull green. 32.3 × 23.1 cm

Provenance: De Paar.

1854–10–20–1330

Copied by Rubens in the Costume Book (no. 2).

4. *Recto:* Studies of various figures of the burgher class: acrobats, onlookers, etc.
Verso: Studies of various figures of ladies and gentlemen

Pen and brown ink. 19.7 × 31.2 cm

1841-12-11-8 (24)

Literature: Hind, 119 (25).

The figures on the *recto* are copied from woodcut illustrations by Hans Weiditz in Petrarch, *Von der Artzney bayder Glück . . .,* Augsburg, H. Steyner, 1532.

Hans Weiditz (active 1518–36)
5. *'Von Einer Vermählelten Braut'* (Concerning a Marriage Settlement)

Woodcut. 10 × 15.5 cm

1897-8-13-10

Illustration in Petrarch, *Von der Artzney bayder Glück . . .,* Augsburg, H. Steyner, 1532, part of which is copied by Rubens in the Costume Book (no.4).

6. Ten studies of ladies

Pen and brown ink. 31.8 × 40.7 cm

1841-12-11-8 (27)

Literature: Hind, 119 (28).

Inscribed by the artist with colour and costume notes.

7. A Castilian lady and servant girl from a village near Pamplona

Pen and brown ink and wash with touches of black, brown, red and yellow chalk. 31.8 × 39.2 cm

1841-12-11-8 (31)

Literature: Hind, 119 (32).

Inscribed by the artist in pen *Dame de Castilla* and *la servante de village hors de Pamplone.*

These studies appear to have been done from the life during the artist's first visit to Spain in 1603.

8. Eight Turkish women

Pen and brown ink. 41.6 × 31.8 cm

1841-12-11-8 (37)

Literature: Hind, 119 (38); H. and O. Kurz, *Nederlands Kunsthistorisch Jaarboek,* Deel xxiii, 1972, pp.275–90.

Inscribed by the artist in pen in connection with the central figure in the lower row, *Sultana;* also notes on the colour and material of the costumes. A later inscription in the margin of the book mistakenly identifies the figures above, with their faces covered, as *Les criminels allant recueiller le poison de l'arbre nommé Bohon upa dans un désert de Java* ('Assassins going to gather poison from the Bohon up a tree in a Javanese desert').

Hilde and Otto Kurz have identified this and other sheets of oriental costume studies in the Costume Book as copies made from replicas derived from the watercolour drawings of Turkish costumes in a volume dated by an

5

8

6

7

anonymous artist, 25 June 1587, Constantinople. It is now in the L. A. Meyer Memorial Library at Jerusalem.

The upper half of the exhibited sheet is an abbreviated copy of a procession of Turkish women going to the Baths. This was almost the only occasion, in fact, when they would have been visible to visiting Europeans. The figure of the woman seated on a carpet on the right is not in the volume at Jerusalem, but occurs elsewhere in similar sources, such as Nicolas de Nicolay's *Les Quatre Premiers Livres des Navigations et Peregrinations Orientales,* Lyon, 1568.

On the lower half of the sheet the girl with the castanets is a gypsy, and the veiled woman, a Jewess. According to Rubens's inscription, the centre figure is the Sultana; but according to Kurz, who bases his opinion on a note in Turkish on the Jerusalem volume, she is neither the mother nor one of the wives of the Sultan, but just a member of the harem. The girl on her right is one of her servants.

9

10

9. Philip I, the Handsome, King of Spain

Pen and brown ink with grey wash. 30.4 × 18.9 cm
Provenance: Friedrich August II, King of Saxony.
1949-5-14-1

10. Joanna the Mad, Queen of Spain

Pen and brown ink with grey wash, parts of the long
sleeves heightened with white bodycolour.
30.4 × 18.7 cm
Provenance: Friedrich August II, King of Saxony.
1949-5-14-2

11. *Recto:* Hero and Leander
Verso: Various sketches

Pen and brown ink and wash; on the *verso,* pen and
brown ink. 20.4 × 30.6 cm
Provenance: P. J. Mariette, possibly a leaf from Rubens's
Pocket Book which had been saved from the fire of 1720.
Edinburgh, National Gallery of Scotland
Literature: M. Jaffé, *MD,* viii, 1970, pp.42–50.

The drawing on the *recto,* inscribed by the artist *Leander
natans Cupidine praevio,* is clearly a first idea for the painting
of *Hero and Leander,* now in Yale University Art Gallery.
Jaffé sees Rubens's management of the waves as a reflection
of Leonardo's 'deluge drawings' which he had recently
seen in Milan. The painting may have been done prior to
his sea-trip to Spain so his depiction of the storm would not
necessarily have owed anything to his first-hand experience. His portrayal of the nymphs is clearly dependent
on Giulio Romano's decorations at Mantua, in particular
his *Hylas being carried off by the Nymphs.*

The principal design on the *verso* is inspired by
Leonardo's *Battle of Anghiari* and is, like the drawing on the
recto, the first idea for a composition, in this case recorded at
a more advanced stage, of Rubens's *Battle of the Amazons* in
the British Museum (no.21). Although the protagonists

11r

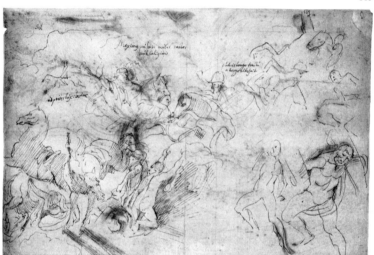

11v

12

here are not engaged in such close combat as in the Edinburgh drawing, there is no mistaking the connection between the two battles. All the inscriptions in Latin on the present drawing which are in the artist's hand refer to natural phenomena. In the lower right-hand corner of the sheet is a figure of Samson, totally unconnected with the battle, which was subsequently copied by Van Dyck in his Antwerp Sketch Book.

Jaffé has proposed a plausible *terminus post quem* for the sheet of 1601–2, on the basis of a stylistic comparison between the fallen Amazon on the left of the Edinburgh *verso* and the Thisbe in the drawing of the *Suicide of Thisbe,* now divided between the Louvre and Bowdoin College, Maine. The Samson on the Edinburgh *verso* presupposes knowledge of the collections of antique sculpture in Rome and in particular of the Farnese Hercules. The dramatic lighting of the Yale painting is inconceivable without first-hand knowledge of Tintoretto's work and as has already been mentioned, the nymphs recall vividly Giulio Romano's at Mantua. The *terminus ante quem* is more difficult to establish. At Rotterdam there is a sheet of studies for a *Martyrdom of St Ursula* probably connected with the painting of that subject at Mantua which can be dated 1604–5. On it there are ideas that can be related to the Yale painting. It is possible but not certain that work on the Yale painting might have been interrupted by the journey to Spain in 1603.

12. The Head of Marie de Médicis

Pen and brown ink. 6.5 × 3.9 cm

Provenance: Sir Joshua Reynolds; R. Payne Knight bequest, 1824.

Oo. 9-21

Literature: Rooses, 1516: Hind, 89; Glück-Haberditzl, 38.

To judge from its style this is an early drawing from Rubens's stay in Italy. This view receives further support from the high dressing of the sitter's hair, which was fashionable at the beginning of the seventeenth century. Rubens was present in Florence at Marie de Médicis's marriage by proxy to Henry IV of France on 5 October 1600, and it is quite likely that the drawing was done on this occasion. The artist attended as a member of the retinue of the Duke of Mantua whose service he had recently entered as a court painter. The Duke of Mantua himself was the husband of the bride's elder sister. It is possible, although there is no positive evidence, that Rubens may have planned as a courtly gesture to add a portrait of Marie to the Duke's collection of pretty women in his 'gallery of beauties' at Mantua.

13. Silenus

Black chalk. 41.9 × 25.6cm
Provenance: William Fawkener bequest.

5211-58
Literature: Hind, 51.

This is a copy after an antique statue of the Drunken Silenus, of which there are important versions at Munich and Dresden. Unfortunately Rubens has left us no note of the location of the pieces of sculpture that he copied. But it seems most likely that he did this drawing after the statue now at Dresden, which, prior to its arrival there in 1728, had been in the Chigi collection in Rome.

14. Two studies of a boy

Red chalk with touches of white bodycolour. The background has been tinted in grey wash by a later hand. 26 × 36cm
Provenance: G. Hugnier; William Fawkener bequest.

5213-1
Literature: Hind, 52; Glück-Haberditzl, 27; Burchard-d'Hulst, 16.
Inscribed in pen by a later hand, lower right, *Rubens*.

These two studies are derived from a late Hellenistic bronze of the first century BC, the famous *Spinario*, now in the Palazzo dei Conservatori, Rome. It is quite likely that Rubens worked not from the original but from a later copy in bronze or a plaster-cast in the studio. The right-hand figure is close to the original, but in the other the artist has turned the boy's head and he is drying his feet instead of extracting a thorn. The pose of this left-hand figure recalls that of Susanna in the painting of *Susanna and the Elders,* now in the Borghese Gallery, executed in Rome about 1606–8. A seated man holding his foot like the *Spinario* also occurs in the *Baptism of Christ,* now in the Antwerp Museum, one of the paintings for S. Trinità, Mantua, a commission completed on 25 May 1605. It is most likely that the present drawing belongs to the artist's first stay in Rome.

15. Head of a weeping bearded man

Pen and brown ink, with a light green tint behind the head. 32 × 19.7cm
Provenance: R. Payne Knight bequest, 1824.

Oo. 9-24
Literature: Hind, 101.
Inscribed in pen by a later hand, lower left, *Rubens*.

This is most probably intended to represent Heraclitus of Ephesus, philosopher and scientist, who lived about 500 BC.

It is quite likely that this is a preparatory study for the head of the weeping Heraclitus in a painting of Democritus and Heraclitus, executed for the Duke of Lerma on the occasion of the artist's first visit to Spain in 1603. This work, whose present whereabouts is not known, is not to be confused with a pair of paintings of the two philosophers, now in Madrid, which were mistakenly assumed to have

13

14

15

been originally joined together. Certainly the vigorous untidy character of the penwork speaks strongly in favour of an early date and is consistent with its being for the Duke of Lerma's painting. The paintings in Madrid are, in fact, much later in date. They belong to the end of Ruben's career and hung in the Torre de la Parada with Velasquez's *Aesop* and *Menippus*.

The opposed attitudes to the human condition of these two philosophers were a contrast attractive to the Renaissance world. This was aptly taken up by Robert Burton, an almost exact contemporary of Rubens in his *Anatomy of Melancholy*. In its foreword, addressed 'to the Mischievously idle reader', we find the following lines of verse:

Weep, Heraclitus, for this wretched age,
Nought dost thou see that is not base and sad;
Laugh on, Democritus, thou laughing sage,
Nought dost thou see that is not vain and bad.
Let one delight in tears and one in laughter,
Each shall find his occasion ever after.

16

17

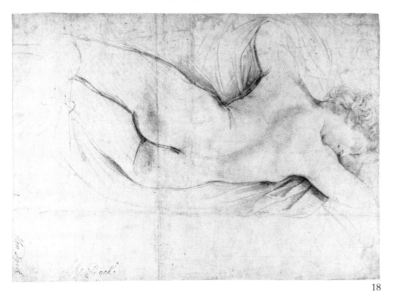

16. Moses and the Brazen Serpent

Black chalk with pen and brown ink, and brown and grey wash, heightened with white bodycolour. Part of the drawing has been done on a mosaic of pieces of paper that have been pasted on to the main sheet.

38.5 × 59.6 cm

Provenance: Sir T. Lawrence; William II, King of Holland; G. Leembruggen; Malcolm.

1895-9-15-1055

Literature: Hind, 4; U. Hoff, *OMD,* xiii, 1938, pp.14–16; G. Fubini and J. S. Held, *MD,* ii, 1964. p.125.

This drawing is made up of figures derived from the *Brazen Serpent* by Michelangelo which decorates a corner-spandrel of the ceiling of the Sistine Chapel. Hind mistakenly saw this drawing as a study for the *Brazen Serpent* of about 1637 in the National Gallery, London. Rather it belongs to an earlier period of the artist's career, and he appears to have had it in mind when painting a much earlier rendering of the *Brazen Serpent,* the painting in the collection of Count Antoine Seilern. This work, formerly thought by some to be by Van Dyck, was most probably executed by Rubens shortly after his return to Antwerp from Italy in December 1608. In the painting the running man occurs again on the left but is reversed. In some other features the painting is more directly connected with Michelangelo's fresco than with this drawing. A drawing in the Ambrosiana in Milan is a copy of the present drawing done before it had been cut down at the bottom and on the right.

17. Mars, Minerva and Iris: an allegory of the city of Brescia

Pen and brown ink. 31.6 × 38.4 cm

Provenance: R. Cosway.

1897-4-10-12

Literature: Hind, 25; R. Baumstark, *Aachener Kunstblätter,* xlv, 1974, p.169.

This is connected stylistically by Hind with the *Battle of the Amazons* in the British Museum collection (no.21) and assigned by him to the artist's stay in Italy. Most authorities accept the attribution to Rubens, with the exception of Horst Vey. He regards Van Dyck as the author because of a supposed stylistic connection with other copies after Titian done by him in Italy, in the Chatsworth Sketchbook, now in the British Museum. Both Burchard and Müller-Hofstede have rightly rejected this view.

Erika Tietze-Conrat *(Arte Veneta,* viii, 1954, pp. 209–10) was the first to trace this composition to its source – the octagon in the centre of the ceiling of the Town Hall at Brescia, a commission ordered from Titian in 1565, completed in 1568 but destroyed in a fire in 1578. The programme for the decoration is fortunately well documented. Evidently Titian does not seem to have executed the work himself. In January 1566 Titian produced two designs for it, one of which is recorded in Cornelis Cort's engraving *The Forge of Cyclops.* Of the other we have only the programme and the detailed account by Zamboni of the subject of the middle panel, which coincides with the British Museum drawing in all respects. The figures shown are Brescia, Minerva, Mars and three Naiads. In the centre is a figure representing Brescia holding a golden statue in her hand and to her left is Minerva holding an olive branch, while Mars stands on the right, a magpie at his feet. The very detailed description leaves no doubt of the connection between the ceiling painting and this drawing, and it seems most likely, as Tietze-Conrat suggests, that Rubens saw a preparatory drawing from Titian's studio for the composition. Hind's suggestion that the Minerva and Iris are copied after the antique is confirmed by the programme's reference to the use of antique coins as models.

18. Sleeping Hermaphrodite

Black chalk. 31 × 43.7 cm

Provenance: Conte de Fries; Sir T. Lawrence; S. Woodburn; Sir T. Phillipps; T. Fitzroy Fenwick; presented anonymously.

1946-7-13-1005

Literature: A. E. Popham, *The Phillipps Fenwick Collection of Drawings,* 1935, p.184, no.3.

Although two early inscriptions on the drawing attribute it to Van Dyck, Rubens is undoubtedly the author of this copy after the antique sculpture in the Borghese collection. Popham's criticism of it as being 'too weak and colourless' for the young Rubens we find it difficult to follow. The general popularity of Hermaphrodite sculpture was due to the prestige of this famous example. It is not clear, however, which if any of the versions surviving is the famous work mentioned by Pliny the Elder as the masterpiece of Polyclitus. Rubens was obviously much impressed by this sculpture as in addition to this vivid rendering he did a second copy, more delicately sketched in black chalk, which is now in a private collection in New York.

19. Demeter or Ceres

Red chalk. 42.1 × 22.6 cm

Provenance: Sir T. Lawrence; S. Woodburn;
Sir T. Phillipps; T. Fitzroy Fenwick; presented
anonymously.

1946-7-13-1004

Literature: A. E. Popham, *The Phillipps Fenwick Collection
of Drawings,* 1935, p.16, no.17 (as Roman? school XVIth
century); Burchard-d'Hulst, under 12; J. Müller-
Hofstede, *Wallraf-Richartz Jahrbuch,* xxvii, 1965, p.270.

Popham thought that this drawing might belong to the
seventeenth century but did not recognize Rubens's hand.
It is, in fact, a copy done by Rubens in Rome after the
statue of Demeter, the Greek corn goddess, formerly in the
collection of Ciriaco Maffei, and since 1770 in the
Vatican. Stylistically the drawing is closely akin to another in the
Lugt collection in Paris, after an antique statue supposedly
of the Emperor Nero, but to be identified with that
of an unknown Roman, now in the British Museum
(inv. no.1943). This was probably formerly in the collection of the Earl of Arundel.

Later in Rubens's career, almost certainly about 1612–15,
this statue made its appearance again in a painting of the
statue of Demeter or Ceres in Leningrad (KdK 83). In this
her white animated figure is represented by Rubens
standing in an elaborate, very solidly built baroque niche.
This painting is notable for being a highly successful
instance of Rubens's collaboration with Frans Snyders. All
the beautifully modelled and highly colourful fruit with
which *putti* are decorating the goddess's shrine have been
painted by Snyders. Both artists at this period had adopted
a similar robust style, which meant their joint productions
were for the most part harmonious entities.

20. *Recto:* The Farnese Bull
Verso: The Farnese Hercules

Black chalk. 22.2 × 26.8 cm

Provenance: v. Ustinov; E. J. Blaiberg bequest.

1970-9-19-103

The drawing on the *recto* was executed by Rubens after
part of the classical group known as the 'Farnese Bull'
representing the punishment of Dirce by her sons, Zethus
and Amphion. It had been dug up in the Baths of Caracella
in the sixteenth century where it had been placed originally
by Asinus Pollio in the time of the Emperor Augustus.
Rubens sketched it in the Palazzo Farnese. In 1786 it was
transported to Naples with the rest of the Farnese collection
of antique sculpture, which also included the Farnese
Hercules. There are two sketches of the latter on the *verso.*

19

20r

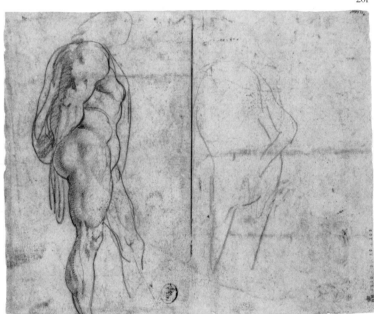

20v

21. Battle of the Amazons

Pen and brown ink over traces of a preliminary drawing in black chalk. 25.2 × 43 cm

Provenance: J. Richardson, senior; E. Bouverie; Sir J. C. Robinson; Malcolm.

1895-9-15-1045

Literature: Rooses, 1458; Hind, 24; Held, 2; Burchard-d'Hulst, 50.

Apart from the obvious influence of classical reliefs, this tightly packed composition reflects Rubens's admiration for Leonardo da Vinci's *Battle of Anghiari*. In the copy, now in the Louvre, that Rubens made from a copy of this lost masterpiece, characteristically he has heightened the drama of the subject by showing one side about to make off with the standard. The fighting horses in the present drawing are a direct quotation from the composition by Leonardo. The *Battle of Anghiari* held a continuing sway subsequently over Rubens in compositions involving mêlées of men and horses. Another drawing in the British Museum collection, also clearly inspired by Leonardo's painting, is the *Battle of the Standard* (no.22).

Rubens appears to have painted this subject, the *Battle of the Amazons,* on at least three occasions. The best known of these is the painting in Munich of about 1618 (KdK 196). In it, however, the present drawing is reflected only in minor details, which include the Amazon holding up the severed head of a Greek, the stumbling horse and the man with a lion skin. Many details from this drawing also are to be found in other paintings. The horse on the left kicking with his hind legs appears both in the *Conversion of St Paul* in Berlin (KdK 155), and in that in the collection of Count Antoine Seilern (KdK 157), formerly in Munich. The latter composition also shows the motif of the horse jumping into the picture over a falling Amazon. This occurs again in the companion painting, still in Munich, the *Defeat of Sennacherib* (KdK 156).

21

RITTER LIBRARY
BALDWIN-WALLACE COLLEGE

22

22. Battle of the Standard

Black chalk with touches of red chalk, reinforced in
places with the brush in brown wash. 41.5 × 52.2 cm
Provenance: P. H. Lankrink; T. Dimsdale;
Sir T. Lawrence; Sir J. C. Robinson; Malcolm.

1895-9-15-1044
Literature; Hind, 21; Glück-Haberditzl, 8.

Inscribed in pen by a later hand, lower right, *P. P. Rubenss.*
Upper left is an autograph inscription in Italian, now so
faint that a few words can be made out: *guarda...
Mediana (?) far si che colui... il Colpo si alsi su piedi sopra le
staffe... avvicinare gli nemici.*

This appears to be an original design by Rubens inspired by
Leonardo's *Battle of Anghiari.* Motifs in this drawing occur
again in the drawing of the *Battle of the Amazons* (no.21),
such as the horse with the flowing mane, and the rearing
horse seen from the front.

23

Gerard Edelinck (1640–1707)

23. Battle of the Standard

Engraving: 44.9 × 60 cm

Provenance: The Rev. C. M. Cracherode.

V-I-88

Literature: Schneevoogt, p.152, no.130.

This print records in reverse the drawing in the Louvre by Rubens of the *Battle of Anghiari* after Leonardo da Vinci. The drawing shows no sign of its outlines having been indented for transfer. Most probably Edelinck worked from his own repetition of Rubens's drawing.

24. *Recto:* Sketches for a Last Supper
Verso: Sketches for Hercules or Saint Sebastian

Pen and brown ink and wash. 28.3 × 44.4 cm

Chatsworth, the Devonshire Collection, (1007)

Literature: Held, under 7; Burchard-d'Hulst, 35.

The studies on this sheet show the influence of Raphael and Leonardo upon the young Rubens. In particular two of the Apostles above right are based on figures in Leonardo's *Last Supper,* which the artist is likely to have seen in Milan before his first visit to Rome in 1600–1. Although inspired by Raphael, the Apostle seen from behind who occurs also in no.25 is closest to the seated young man in Caravaggio's *Calling of St Matthew.*

In line with his dramatic style at this early part of his career Rubens has chosen to depict the *Last Supper* at the moment when Jesus has been called upon to reveal who will betray him.

There is no agreement as to whether Rubens intended the figure studies on the *verso* to be Hercules or St Sebastian tied to a tree. Whatever Rubens's intention was, the figures are strongly dependent on the Laocoön group sculpture.

24r

24v

25. *Recto:* Sketches for a Last Supper
Verso: Medea and her slain children

Pen and brown ink. 29.3 × 43.4 cm

Chatsworth, the Devonshire Collection, (1006)

Literature: Held, 7; Burchard-d'Hulst, 34.

Inscribed by the artist in pen, upper right, *Gestus magis largi longiq[ue] brachijs extensis,* and on the *verso,* upper right, *vel Medea respiciens Creusam ardentem et Jasonem velut[? Inseg...]*

Although reflecting the influence of Caravaggio's *Calling of St Matthew* in San Luigi dei Francesi in Rome and Marcantonio Raimondi's engraving after Raphael of the *Last Supper,* these studies are the highly original product of Rubens's inventive genius. They are an eloquent indication of the heightened dramatic power that the young artist had in him at the commencement of his career. There is no conclusive evidence to support the idea that Rubens produced a painting of the Last Supper based on these sketches, but there are undeniable connections between this sheet and another sheet of studies also at Chatsworth (no.24) and some of Rubens's early paintings. The types of the Apostles have much in common with the series, now in Madrid, painted in 1603. The exaggerated drama of the figures in both the Chatsworth sheets recalls those in the *Transfiguration* of 1605, now at Nancy (KdK 15), painted for S. Trinità at Mantua. This large painting is a not entirely successful attempt to transpose Raphael's famous painting into the baroque idiom. The tearful Apostle in the present sheet should be compared with the study for Rubens's *Weeping Heraclitus* (no.15), evidently done on his first visit to Spain, while the bearded man on the left in the lower row of Apostles might almost be considered a sketch for the man supporting the possessed child in the *Transfiguration.* His features are certainly very similar. The tension of high drama is also not absent from the sketches of Medea on the *verso.* Here Rubens has presented us with the full measure of the despairing mother's anguish. The dead child represented in the centre of the sheet has evidently been drawn after one of Niobe's daughters on a classical sarcophagus.

25r

25v

26. Study for a standing female saint

Brush and light brown wash over traces of black chalk; certain contours reinforced in pen and dark brown ink. 46.7 × 30.9 cm

Provenance: L. Burchard, who had acquired it in Rome in 1932.

New York, Metropolitan Museum of Art (65.175)

Literature: H. G. Evers, *Rubens und sein Werk, neue Forschungen,* 1943, pp.107–119; Held, 74; Burchard-d'Hulst, 28.

Inscribed crudely in pen by a later hand, upper left, *Antonius Van Dyck,* and, lower left, *A.V.D.*

As Burchard has observed, this full-length female figure, seen partly from behind, resembles both in dress and attitude classical marble statues of Roman Empresses. The addition of the sword, however, as an afterthought—the hilt is drawn over the hand which is meant to be grasping

26

27

it—suggests that the figure is intended to be a saint or martyr. It is, in fact, a drawing for St Domitilla, made in connection with the preparation of the first version, now at Grenoble, of Rubens's most important Roman commission, the high altarpiece for the Chiesa Nuova. Although there is some disagreement amongst the authorities as to the precise order in which the various drawings and oil-sketches for this commission were made, the present drawing fortunately can be specifically connected with a pen and ink study, formerly also in the collection of Ludwig Burchard. This rapidly drawn sketch records the artist's initial and later largely rejected ideas for the disposition and poses of the saints that were to be ranged in the picture before the archway, over which hangs an image of the Virgin and Child. In the first painting the pose of St Domitilla is radically changed from her representation in Rubens's initial drawings. Because of the close similarity of the pose of the Saint in the sketch, formerly in the Burchard collection (inspired by Titian's woodcut *The Six Saints*) to that in the present drawing, it is clear that this masterly brush drawing too was originally intended by Rubens to serve as a preparatory study for St Domitilla. Her representation in the painting at Grenoble, in fact, anticipates in a general way the appearance of St Catherine on the back of one of the wings of the *Raising of the Cross,* now in Antwerp Cathedral (KdK 36). The oil-sketches for the backs of both wings of this triptych are in the Dulwich College Gallery (nos. 55, 56).

27. St Ignatius pleading before Pope Julius III for the establishment of a Jesuit college in Rome

Pen and brown ink and wash, heightened with white bodycolour. 11.6 × 10.3 cm

Provenance: P. J. Mariette; David Laing; Royal Scottish Academy; transferred to the National Gallery of Scotland, 1910.

Edinburgh, National Gallery of Scotland (D.1695)

Literature: J. S. Held, *MD*, xii, 1974, pp.249–60.

A preparatory drawing for an anonymous engraving in the *Vita Beati P. Ignatii,* 1609. It is one of three drawings, once owned by Mariette, that it can be claimed on stylistic grounds Rubens executed for illustrations in this publication. That of *St Ignatius kneeling in a landscape* had previously been found by J. S. Held among the anonymous Flemish drawings in the Louvre (see J. S. Held, 'Rubens and the Vita Beati P. Ignatii Loiolae of 1609' in *Rubens before 1620,* 1972, p.94). The third drawing has yet to be found.

Ignatij in Septemtrionis res apprime intenti
studio, ac precibus Iulius III.Pont.Max.Collegium
Germaniæ iuuentutis non minori Ecclesiæ Romanæ
ornamento,quam Germaniæ præsidio Romæ condit.
64

28

Anonymous engraver

28. St Ignatius pleading before Pope Julius III
for the establishment of a German Jesuit college
in Rome

Engraving. 14.9 × 9.7 cm
The British Library, Department of Printed Books

Rubens provided the preparatory design for this illustration, plate 64 in *Vita Beati P. Ignatii,* Rome, 1609
(no.27).

29. Portrait of Marchesa Brigida Spinola Doria

Pen and brown ink and wash over black chalk; folds of
the drapery emphasized with black chalk. 31.5 × 18.5 cm
Provenance: E. Schilling; private collection, New York.
New York, Pierpont Morgan Library, (1975.28)
Literature: Held, 73.

This drawing is evidently the sole surviving preparatory
drawing for a portrait from Rubens's visit to Genoa when
he painted a whole series of portraits of the Genoese
nobility. The portrait itself was painted in 1606 at Genoa,
when the sitter married Massimiliano Doria. The painting,
which is in the National Gallery of Art, Washington D.C.,
has been cut down so that the sitter now appears three-
quarter length. From a lithograph of 1848 we know that it
was then a full-length portrait.

Rubens has made various notes on the drawing in

Flemish: *hout* (wood) on the cornice; *goudt* (gold) below the
first capital; *root* (red) on the curtain. All these directions he
followed in the painting.

30a. St Domitilla, St Nereus, and St Achilleus

Pen and brown ink and brown wash. 15.3 × 13.3 cm
Provenance: P. J. Mariette; Marquis de Lagoy;
Sir T. Lawrence; Malcolm.
1895-9-15-1060
Literature: Hind, 14 (as by Van Dyck after Rubens);
Glück-Haberditzl, 52; J. S. Held, *Rubens before 1620,*
1972, p.98.
Inscribed in pen by a later hand, lower right, *A.V.D.*

This and the following drawing mounted with it have been
variously described by scholars in the past. Hind regarded
both as free copies by Van Dyck based on Rubens's Chiesa
Nuova altarpiece finished in October 1608. Glück-
Haberditzl accepted them as by Rubens and as sketches for
this commission. Held has recently discussed the present
drawing in connection with a drawing in the Louvre
which he has identified as for an engraving in a Life of
St Ignatius published in Rome in 1609 (see nos.27,28). The
British Museum drawing is considered by Held to be a
study for the right-hand part of the altarpiece produced as a
substitute in 1608 following the abandonment of the first
painted version finished in June 1607, now in Grenoble
(KdK 23). It had been rejected by the Oratorian Fathers
because reflections prevented one from seeing the painting
properly.

Rubens radically redesigned the altarpiece. Instead of a
single canvas with the sacred painting of the Virgin and
Child above an arch, below which saints are grouped, the
composition is spread over three panels of slate, a material
used to avoid disturbing reflections. The central panel
contains a tabernacle for the sacred painting, surrounded
by a host of worshipping angels. On each of the side panels
are grouped three saints. Those in the present drawing
correspond but, by no means slavishly, with the saints on
the right, and those in the following drawing (no.30b) with
the saints on the left.

There is a preparatory drawing for the central panel in
the Albertina (Glück-Haberditzl, 54), which in its pen
work is closely allied to the present drawing. The same
kinship does not, however, extend to the other British
Museum drawing which at first sight appears to be a
companion to it. Despite the fact that the provenance of the
two drawings is identical, one is bound to question the
status of this second drawing which has been described by
Glück-Haberditzl as an early idea for the second altarpiece
on slate. It was considered as earlier than the sketch at
Chantilly (Glück-Haberditzl, 53) which is closer than it in
its proportions to the final painting. This second drawing
(no.30b) lacks the vigour of Rubens, and technically,
particularly in the application of the washes, has no parallel
elsewhere in Rubens's early drawings. Hind attributed it to
Van Dyck on the strength of the inscription, which he took
to be a signature.

29

30a

30b. St Gregory, St Maurus, and St Papianus

Pen and brown ink and wash, heightened with white
bodycolour over black chalk. 15.3 × 13.3 cm

Provenance: The same as for no.30a.

1895-9-15-1061

Literature: Hind, 15 (as by Van Dyck after Rubens);
Glück-Haberditzl, 51.

Inscribed in pen by a later hand, lower left, *A. Van Dyck.*

For discussion of this drawing see above, no.30a.

30b

Copies after other Masters

Until recently, great emphasis was laid upon copying as a means of educating an artist. Rubens attached particular importance to this practice and continued to copy throughout his career. Furthermore, in Italy he was commissioned by the Duke of Mantua and others to paint a number of copies after Italian sixteenth-century masterpieces. The drawn copies, made largely for his own benefit, allow us to assess his personal taste and to see which artists had the profoundest effect on his own creations. Apart from the copies after the antique (for which see nos.95-139) his interest in art before the sixteenth century seems to have been primarily archaeological, enabling him to invest his paintings of historical subjects with reasonably authentic costumes and settings. Nevertheless, he copied after a wide range of diverse artistic personalities. His chief interest lay in the work of the greatest Italian draughtsmen of the preceding century, above all in those who composed in the classical style: Leonardo, Michelangelo, Raphael and the latter's followers, Giulio Romano, Perino del Vaga, Polidoro da Caravaggio and the more contemporary Annibale Carracci (1560-1609). Most of the copies after these masters naturally date from the Italian Period, when Rubens was probably concerned to build up a stock of what were, for him, reproductions of the finest Italian masterpieces, recorded at first hand, to which he could refer at any time in the future (cf. nos.37,38).

Rubens's interest in northern artists was probably as intense, although fewer copies of them exist, presumably because he could study northern originals in Antwerp. Those shown here, after three very different artists (Jacob Cornelisz Cobaert, Peter Brueghel the Elder and Adam Elsheimer, nos.34,40,41) reveal the same concern with particular figures or sections of the compositions under study as we see in those after Italian masters. Whatever the source, the copies are never slavish, but are executed with a critical eye and translated into Rubens's own visual language, ready to be adapted if necessary to one of his own compositions.

Rubens ? after Perino del Vaga (1501–47)
31. Nessus and Deianira
Pen and brown ink and wash with green, brown and white bodycolour. 25.2 × 20.3 cm. Arched top.
Provenance: J. Richardson, senior; Earl of Aylesford.
1893-7-31-19
Literature: Hind, 46; P. Pouncey and J. A. Gere, *Italian Drawings . . . in the British Museum: Raphael and his Circle,* 1962, no.196.
Inscribed in lower left-hand corner, in ink, *Perinus del Vaga.*

Hind suggests that this is a lightly drawn original by Perino del Vaga which has been thoroughly reworked by Rubens. The opinion of Pouncey and Gere that the drawing is entirely by Rubens, probably after a composition of Perino's, seems a more reasonable view to take.

Rubens after Polidoro da Caravaggio (1499/1500–?1543)
32. A man leading a horse (*see colour plate page 51*)
Brush drawing in brown with some pen and ink heightened with white bodycolour. 42.7 × 23.5 cm
Provenance: P. H. Lankrink; Sir J. C. Robinson; Malcolm. 1895-9-15-653
Literature: Hind 47; P. Pouncey and J. A. Gere, *Italian Drawings . . . in the British Museum: Raphael and his Circle,* 1962, no.225.

This is a copy by Rubens after a detail of the frieze by Polidoro da Caravaggio, immediately above the ground floor on the facade of the Palazzo Milesi in the Via della Maschera d'Oro, Rome. Now only traces of the decoration are to be seen. But fortunately the decorative scheme, and in particular the frieze, were much copied, and it was engraved by G. B. Galestruzzi and J. Sanraedam amongst others.

Rubens after Raphael (1483–1520)
33. A naked man dropping from a wall
Pen and brown ink with brown wash and white bodycolour. 22.5 × 11.1 cm
Provenance: R. Payne Knight bequest, 1824.
Oo.9–23
Literature: Hind, 49; P. Pouncey and J. A. Gere, *Italian Drawings . . . in the British Museum: Raphael and his Circle,* 1962, under no.87.

This is a copy after a figure from Raphael's fresco, the *Fire in the Borgo,* in the Stanza dell'Incendio in the Vatican. It appears, however, as Pouncey and Gere have pointed out, that it is a copy drawn not directly from the fresco itself, but from a lost copy of it. For the figure differs from the fresco in having no drapery, in the position of its right arm, and in the shadow it casts. Rubens's copy shares all these features with two other drawn copies from the Raphael School after this figure, one in the Albertina, Vienna and the other in the Ashmolean Museum, Oxford.

31

32

33

Rubens after Jacob Cornelisz Cobaert (active 1568–1615)

34. Three of the nymphs of Diana undressing

Pen and brown ink over black chalk. 17.2 × 14.7 cm

Provenance: G. Knapton; General Morrison; W. Y. Ottley; R. Payne Knight bequest, 1824.

Oo.9-54

Literature: Hind, 26 (as by Van Dyck); Burchard-d'Hulst, 11.

This is one of two surviving sketches by Rubens, the other being at Chatsworth (inv. no. 1013), of details from two relief plaquettes by Jacob Cornelisz Cobaert. These plaquettes are from a series of eight oval and eight octagonally cut reliefs, of which many replicas and copies exist, illustrating scenes from Ovid's Metamorphoses.

The present drawing is a study of the three principal nymphs on the left-hand side of the composition in the plaque of *Diana and Callisto* (see no. 35). The study at Chatsworth is of four of the Bacchantes seated around the table in *King Midas celebrating the arrival of the Silenus*.

Jacob Cornelisz Cobaert, also called 'Coppe Fiammingo' (active 1568–1615), after Guglielmo della Porta (active 1531–77)

35. Diana and Callisto

Octagonal bronze plaque. 13.5 × 13.5 cm

Provenance: Presented by Dr. W. L. Hildburgh.

London, Victoria and Albert Museum (A.87–1937)

Literature: L. Planiscig, *Kunsthistorisches Museum in Wien, Die Estensische Kunstsammlung,* i, *Skulpturen und Plastiken,* Vienna, 1919, pp. 188–92; R. Berliner, *Archiv für Medaillen und Plaketten-Kunde,* iii, 1921/2, pp. 134–5; M. Gibellino Krasceninnicowa, *Guglielmo della Porta,* Rome, 1944, pp. 53–55; W. Gramberg, *Jahrbuch der Hamburger Kunstsammlungen,* v, 1960, pp. 31–52.

This plaque was cut from one of a set of sixteen (eight oval and eight octagonal) reliefs with subjects from Ovid's Metamorphoses, designed about 1550–60 by Guglielmo della Porta in Rome and modelled in clay under his supervision by his Flemish assistant Jacob Cobaert. The series was widely known on both sides of the Alps in the late sixteenth and early seventeenth centuries, as a result of the theft of the models from Guglielmo's workshop after his death and their sale by his disinherited son Fidia, who was tried and executed in 1586. In 1609, Teodoro della Porta, Guglielmo's younger son and heir, brought an action against Antonio da Faenza and other Roman goldsmiths for the illegal reproduction of these models. Bronze casts of widely varying quality are in the Victoria and Albert Museum and many other public collections; however, only in the Kunsthistorisches Museum in Vienna is there a complete set. A bronze cast of one of the plaques signed by Fidia della Porta is in the Metropolitan Museum, New York, and two of Cobaert's original fired clay models are in the Victoria and Albert Museum. For a drawing by Rubens after a detail of this plaque, see no. 34.

34

35

36

Rubens after Giulio Romano (*c*.1499–1546)
36. A Roman Triumph

Red chalk, heightened with white bodycolour. The
corners of the drawing have been damaged and made up.
43.8 × 57.5 cm

1972 U.675

Provenance: Possibly S. Woodburn, 1854.

Literature: Hind, 50; M. Jaffé, *The Art Bulletin,* xl,
1958, p.329, no.II.

This is a free copy, in reverse, of one of the *Triumph of Scipio*
drawings by Giulio Romano, now in the Louvre
(inv. no.3549), made as designs for a series of tapestry
cartoons (see F. Hartt, *Giulio Romano,* 1958, i, cat.no.259,
and ii, fig.474).

37

38a

38

Rubens after Michelangelo (1475–1564)
37. Ignudo turning towards the right *(see colour plate page 104)*
Red chalk with a few touches of the brush in red wash.
38.9 × 27.8 cm
Provenance: P. H. Lankrink; E. Bouverie.
1870-8-13-882
Literature: Held, 158; M. Jaffé, *Burlington Magazine*, xcix, 1957 p.376; Burchard-d'Hulst, 18.

Apart from the emphasizing of the muscles, this is a faithful copy of the *Ignudo* between Jonah and the Libyan Sybil on the ceiling of the Sistine Chapel. Although smaller in scale than the series of copies of the Prophets and Sybils now in the Louvre, it clearly has been drawn like these, directly from the fresco and not after engravings. It must therefore have been done during one of Rubens's stays in Rome at the beginning of his career. The style is consonant also with that of other drawings from this early period, such as the *Two Studies of a Boy* (no.14), a work probably from the artist's first stay in Rome.

Rubens after Michelangelo (1475–1564)
38. Ignudo turning towards the left
Red chalk with brush work in several shades of red, heightened with white bodycolour. 32 × 19.8 cm
Provenance: P. H. Lankrink; E. Bouverie.
1870-8-13-883
Literature: Held, under 158; Burchard-d'Hulst, 19.

This is a counterproof of the *Ignudo turning towards the right* (no.37) reworked by the artist with the brush. As the piece of paper he has used is a little too small, Rubens had to make a separate drawing of the right-hand foot, the end of which is missing, between the Ignudo's legs. Rubens has freely modified the figure and details in the composition. The drapery lying over the shoulder has been changed into a garland of oak leaves and he has also added a drapery over the seat. Burchard-d'Hulst's dating of the drawing about 1630–33 is quite plausible as the figure was used by Rubens for that of Bounty in the Whitehall ceiling. On the oil sketch for this in the collection of Count Antoine Seilern the garland has been transformed into a cornucopia. Various changes of pose have also been made. Further reflections of this drawing are to be found in the figure of Juno in the sketch of *Psyche* (KdK 366) in the Liechtenstein collection, and in the figure of Pluto in *Orpheus and Eurydice* in the Prado (KdK 389).

Rubens after Giovanni Angelo Montorsoli (?1507–63)

38a. Pan reclining

Red chalk with red and grey washes heightened with bodycolour over traces of black chalk. 30.9 × 49.3 cm

Provenance: J. Richardson, senior; B. West; Sir C. Greville; Earl of Warwick; C. A. de Burlet; L. Burchard; W. Burchard.

London, P. & D. Colnaghi & Co. Ltd.

Literature: Glück-Haberditzl, 25; Burchard-d'Hulst, 161.

This drawing is a study freely based on Montorsoli's statue which Rubens must have seen in Rome. Pan's features and much of the pose clearly derive from this marble, which was formerly in the Palazzo Barberini in Rome, and is now in the City Art Museum, St Louis. Although the fact that the subject has been reversed might suggest that Rubens may have worked from an engraving, it is quite likely that the drawing may be a highly elaborated reworking of a counterproof, as Burchard-d'Hulst have suggested. One cannot, however, verify this by reference to the original. At any rate, the drawing undoubtedly does have stylistic affinities with another counterproof, the *Ignudo turning towards the left* (no.38), which suggests that possibly the present drawing like it was executed in the early 1630s.

Rubens after Primaticcio (1504/5–70)

39. Telemachos washing the hands and feet of his men

Brush drawing with bodycolour and wash in various colours. 29.3 × 42.9 cm

Provenance: David Laing; Royal Scottish Academy; transferred to the National Gallery of Scotland, 1910.

Edinburgh, National Gallery of Scotland (D.1677)

This is a copy of one of Primaticcio's paintings in the Galerie d'Ulysse at Fontainbleau. The drawing was formerly attributed to Jordaens, no doubt on the grounds of a supposed connection with that artist's highly coloured drawings in bodycolour.

Rubens after Pieter Bruegel the Elder (active 1551–69)

40. A peasant

Black chalk, strengthened with pen and brown ink.
19.8 × 9 cm
Provenance: Hon. Henry Hobhouse.

1935-12-14-4
Literature: M. Jaffé, *MD,* iv, 1966, p.134.

This is a copy by Rubens, after Pieter Bruegel, of one of the leading figures in the procession in the *Village Wedding,* of which the best surviving version is the painting formerly in the collection of Captain E.G. Spencer-Churchill, and now in the Musée Municipal, Brussels. Two other less good versions of the painting exist, one in the Antwerp Museum and the other in a private collection. Among all the drawn copies after Pieter Bruegel the Elder, this is perhaps one of the most convincing of those that have been attributed to Rubens.

Rubens after Adam Elsheimer (1578–1610)

41. A Turkish prince on horseback with attendants

Pen and brown ink and grey wash, with touches of red and yellow chalk. 27.1 × 21.1 cm
Provenance: R. Payne Knight bequest, 1824.

Oo.9-30
Literature: Hind, 44; I. Jost, *Burlington Magazine,*
cviii, 1966, pp.3–6.

In this drawing Rubens has copied and freely arranged figures from Elsheimer's *The Stoning of St Stephen,* a painting discovered relatively recently and now in the National Gallery of Scotland, Edinburgh. An engraving by Pieter Soutman (no.42) reproduces the design of the present drawing in reverse. There is little doubt that Rubens, who greatly admired Elsheimer's work, made his adaptation when he was working in Rome, and would have been in touch with the artist and have had access to his studio. Elsheimer's premature death in December 1610 affected Rubens deeply, as we know from a letter of 14 January 1611 to Jacob Faber, a German doctor in Rome. Of it he says: 'Surely, after such a loss, our entire profession ought to clothe itself in mourning. It will not easily succeed in replacing him; in my opinion he had no equal in small figures, in landscapes, and in many other subjects.' Rubens was not without his criticisms of the young artist, whom he describes as slothful. From Sandrart, a reliable source, we learn that he brooded over his work. His inclination to melancholy was further aggravated by domestic worries and the problem of providing for his many children.

40

42

41

Pieter Soutman (active 1619–57)

42. A Turkish prince on horseback with attendants

Engraving. 29.1 × 21.5 cm (Subject)

Provenance: Marchese J. Durazzo.

1873-8-9-819

Literature: Schneevoogt, 145.76. Second state.

Inscribed on the first state *Adam Elsheimer Invent. Cum Privil.* This is altered on the second state to read *P.P. Rub[ens] pinxit. Cum Privil P. Soutman fecit et Excud.* This print is almost the same size as Rubens's design (no.41) and almost identical, except for the half figure of a man, which may have been cut off in the drawing, walking by the horse's head on the left in the far background.

43

44

Marcantonio Raimondi (*c.*1480–1527/34)
43. Pan and Syrinx
Engraving. 24.9 × 17.2 cm
1863-7-25-1545
Literature: Bartsch, xiv, 245.325. First state.

Rubens after Marcantonio Raimondi
(*c.*1480–1527/34)
44. Pan and Syrinx
Red chalk with brush work in various shades of red.
21.8 × 17.4 cm
Provenance: P. H. Lankrink; J. Richardson, senior; Salting bequest.
1910-2-12-192
Literature: Hind, 28; M. Jaffé, 'Rubens and Raphael', in *Studies . . . presented to A. Blunt,* 1967, pp.99–100.

This is a free adaptation by Rubens in reverse of the first state of the engraving, *Pan and Syrinx,* by Marcantonio Raimondi (no.43).

Opposite
94. Detail from a drawing connected with the 'Fall of the Damned'
71 × 47.5 cm

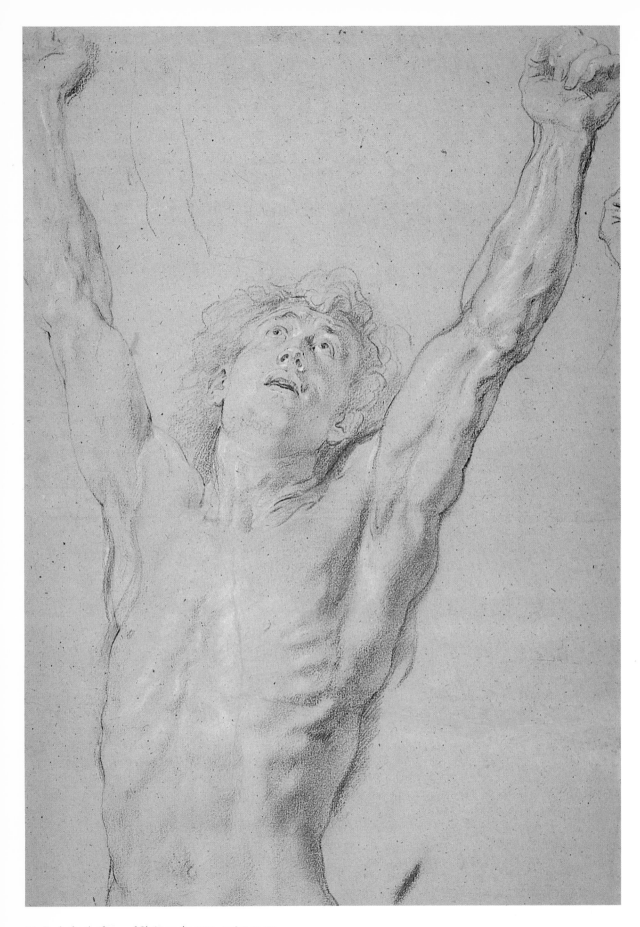

64. Study for the figure of Christ on the cross. 52.8 × 37 cm.

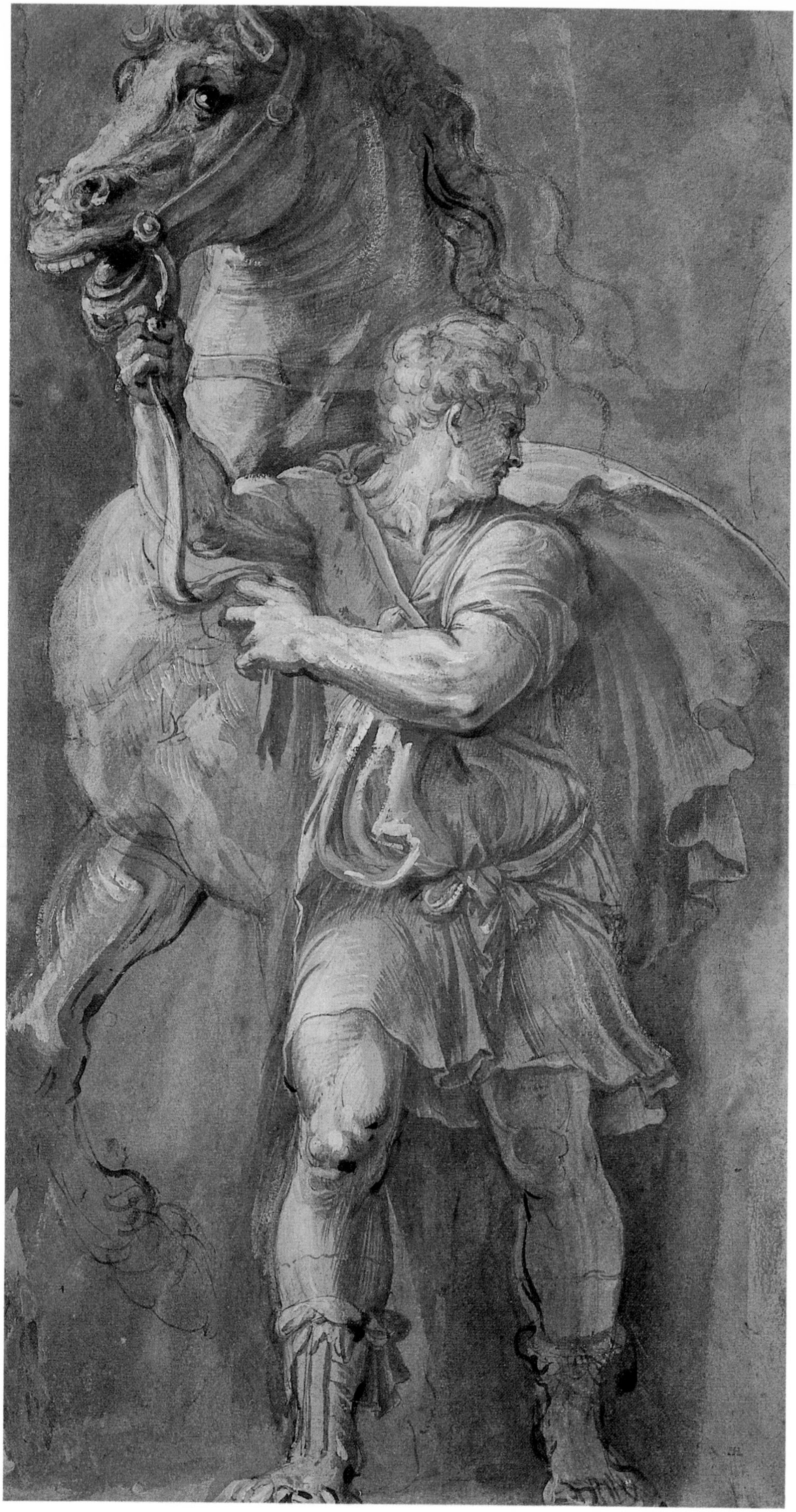

32. A man leading a horse.
42.7 × 23.5 cm.

72. Hercules victorious over Discord.
47.5 × 32 cm.

45

Drawings retouched by Rubens

Collectors have always been aware of Rubens's practice of reworking studies by other masters. In recent years many drawings in this category have been identified. Rubens usually did such reworking in bodycolour, but also occasionally used pen and ink, as for instance in the case of the substantial alterations he made to the offset of a glass-painting design by Hans Holbein the Younger (no.48). Although we might perhaps regard such tampering as amounting to little short of vandalism, an examination of the results on display will, we believe, soon quieten any objections. In many instances Rubens has decidedly enriched what he modified. His motive was sometimes to repair and preserve a damaged drawing. A good example of this is the anonymous copy after part of the decoration of the Farnese Gallery (no.52), which he has repaired and extensively reworked. Some drawings were weak copies, such as that after Paolo Veronese (no.54), until transformed by the magic of Rubens's brush. Retouching by other artists is not unknown, but few could adapt their own styles to that of the originals so successfully.

Copy after Giovanni Bellini (*c*.1430–1516) retouched by Rubens

45. Two Saints

Drawn with the point of the brush on blue surface, heightened with white. 28.1 × 14.2 cm

Provenance: Sir P. P. Rubens; P. J. Mariette; Abbé Gersaint; R. Payne Knight bequest, 1824.

Oo.-9-31

Literature: A. E. Popham, *OMD*, i, 1926–7, p.47; A. E. Popham and P. Pouncey, *Italian Drawings . . . in the British Museum: The XIVth and XVth Centuries*, 1950, no.20.

This is most probably an early copy of the figures on the right-hand wing of Bellini's triptych of 1488 in the Frari church, Venice. It is very likely, as Mariette proposes in the inscription on the mount, that Rubens was responsible for the reworking of this drawing. This is so extensive that it is difficult to make out the character of the original drawing beneath.

Anonymous, Flemish, 15th century, retouched
by Rubens

46. *Recto:* Two studies of draperies
Verso: Two further studies

Pen and light brown ink, partly retouched with a brush
in brown ink. 13.3 × 13.4 cm

The drawing was evidently divided at an early date as
Lankrink put his stamp on both parts.

Provenance: Sir P. P. Rubens; P. H. Lankrink; Sloane
bequest, 1753.

5237-92, 93

Literature: A. E. Popham, *OMD,* i, 1926, p.46; *ibid., Dutch
and Flemish Drawings in the British Museum,* V,
1932, p.63, no.7.

These drawings were considered by Popham as most
probably studies for *pleurers* or mourners. The mantles
worn by the figures are exactly similar to those worn at the
funerals of the great. As they appear to be preliminary
studies from the model this could account for the absence
of the characteristic hoods. Another possibility is that the
figures might represent members of an order of chivalry.

As Popham has pointed out, the hand of the Flemish
draughtsman, active in the last quarter of the 15th century,
is close to that of another drawing also in the British
Museum. This is the *Virgin and Child appearing to St George,*
a design for a three-light window, probably one of a series
of the life of the saint. It was formerly connected with the
miniaturist Philippe de Mazerolles (active 1454 to after
1479) but is now associated with Lieven van Latham, who
had become master at Ghent in 1454. He subsequently
moved to Antwerp where he died in 1493. Popham
suggested that the retouching of the present sheet was
probably by Rubens. If we had to rely just on the
retouching on the *verso* the identity of the retoucher would
have had to remain a matter of speculation. But with that
on the *recto* reflecting Rubens's character so strongly, in our
view there can be no doubt that he is responsible.

Albrecht Dürer (1471–1528) retouched by
Rubens

47. Ecce homo

Pen and brown ink. 26.5 × 18 cm

Provenance: Sir P. P. Rubens.

England, Private Collection

Literature: E. Schilling, 'Werkzeichnungen Dürers zur
"Grünen Passion"' in *Berliner Museen, Berichte a.d. Ehem.
Preussischen Kunstsammlungen,* NF. iv Heft 1/2,
1954, pp.14-24.

Dürer's monogram added by a later hand.

This drawing is probably the last in a series of preparatory
studies for one of the scenes in the 'Grüne Passion'
(Winkler, *Dürers Zeichnungen,* ii, no.308). A study of the
same kind for *Christ carrying the Cross* is in the Berlin Print
Room (Winkler, *op.cit.,* no.309) and another for the
Nailing of Christ to the Cross is in the collection of
Mrs G. Springell (Winkler, *op.cit.,* no.311).

46r

47

46v

48

Hans Holbein the Younger (1497/8–1543) reworked by Rubens

48. Christ carrying the Cross

Offset of drawing in pen and black ink, retouched by Holbein himself with the point of the brush in black ink. In important areas of the composition later retouched and altered by Rubens in pen and brown ink and wash heightened with grey and white bodycolour, with some outlines in pen and black ink. 37.6 × 27.8 cm

Provenance: Sir P. P. Rubens; Joachim von Sandrart; G. F. Fagel; William Y. Ottley; Sir T. Lawrence. 1846-9-18-5

Literature: J. von Sandrart, *Teutsche Academie...,* 1675 (edited Peltzer, 1925), pp.102,333; A. Woltmann, *Holbein und seine Zeit,* Leipzig, 1874, 181; A. B. Chamberlain, *Hans Holbein the Younger,* London, i, 1913, p.156.

One of the offsets taken from the series of Hans Holbein the Younger's ten stained-glass-window designs of the Passion at Basel (Ganz, 169–178) retouched with the brush by the artist. Sandrart, to whom they belonged, called them in his *Teutsche Academie* 'An excellent large Passion in pen, ink and wash, of an amazingly beautiful invention on nine large sheets'. He had, however, only managed to acquire seven of these, for elsewhere in his book he tells his readers that he would be glad to give two hundred guilders for the two which he knew had earlier gone into other hands so that, as he thought, he could show the Passion complete to interested amateurs. From this it is evident that Sandrart was unaware of the existence of the ten drawings at Basel, and that his own drawings were in fact offsets. One should perhaps note also that the set at Basel is almost certainly incomplete as several episodes from the Passion, such as the Agony in the Garden, the Arrest of Christ, Christ before Hannas, the Deposition and the Entombment are all missing. The two offsets for which Sandrart made his offer have never come to light, and his extant offsets have always, it seems, remained together.

The earliest mention of the fact that this offset has been retouched and reworked by Rubens occurs in the relevant entry in T. Philipe's sale catalogue of the Ottley collection in June 1814 (see above), where it was also stated that the seven drawings are those that had belonged to Sandrart. Chamberlain, not recognising Rubens's hand, subsequently described the additional retouchings in sepia as those of 'a later and weaker hand, which greatly mar the design'. Rubens certainly made substantial changes to the two principal protagonists in the composition, Christ and his executioner. The chief changes he made are the lowering of Christ's left arm, and the elimination of his foot. The effect of these alterations is that Christ no longer has control of the cross and is sinking under its weight. Christ's body has been given an exaggerated twist, and this together with the addition of fluttering draperies has given the figure a baroque character. An area in the right-hand background of the offset, which Holbein did not trouble to complete, has not taken properly. Rubens has however noticed there the absence of the heads of two background figures and these he has made good after the manner of such figures in Dürer's woodcuts, in particular those in the 'Little Passion'.

Bernard van Orley (*c*.1488–1541) and Rubens
49. A hawking party

Pen and brown ink and brown wash, with touches of oil colour. 40.4 × 30.8 cm

Provenance: Sir P. P. Rubens; P. H. Lankrink; Sloane bequest, 1753.

5237-77

Literature: Hind, 32; A. E. Popham, *OMD*, i, 1926–27, p.45ff; *ibid., Dutch and Flemish Drawings in the British Museum*, v, 1932, p.227, no.4A.

A sixteenth-century drawing, executed on a square piece of paper, has been enlarged to the left and below on an L-shaped piece by a later artist, who is undoubtedly Rubens. The original agrees in reverse with a group of figures in a tapestry called *Le bat l'eau*, representing the month of September, from a series illustrating the months, known as *Les belles chasses de Maximilian*, designed by van Orley, and a team of collaborators, including Jan Tons, Jacob Tseraerts, Jan van Coninxloo and Pieter Coecke van Aelst.

A set of this series of tapestries is preserved at the Louvre as well as a complete set of preliminary drawings for them, all executed by van Orley himself in the same sense as the tapestries. These drawings are not in any respect cartoons, as these would, apart from the discrepancy of size, have to be in reverse. The cartoons, kept by van Orley's descendants, were destroyed in a French bombardment of Brussels in 1695 (see R. A. d'Hulst, *Tapisseries Flamandes du XVIe au XVIIIe Siècle,* 1960, no.20).

In its original condition, before retouching and enlargement by Rubens, the drawing was evidently the only surviving fragment from an intermediate stage in the design of the tapestries, probably executed by van Orley himself. Another group of drawings, the same size as the drawings in the Louvre, which could be the remnants of another set have been variously described as copies and originals. Of these certainly the drawing at Budapest and the newly discovered *June* at Berlin are lively sketches and it is most probable that these and the two at Leiden, one of which is of *September*, are also by van Orley.

On another occasion it appears Rubens was stimulated by a tapestry design of van Orley's (see L. von Baldass, *Die Wiener Gobelinsammlung,* 1920, pl.12). This interest we find reflected in a burial scene on the *verso* of a drawing of *Studies of St Gregory and St Domitilla,* formerly in the collection of Ludwig Burchard (Burchard-d'Hulst, 26r, and v.).

Copy after Giulio Romano (*c*.1499–1546) reworked by Rubens
50. Perseus disarming, and the origin of coral

Pen and brown ink, reworked by Rubens in brown, yellow and grey washes, heightened with white bodycolour, partly oxidised on faded blue paper.

25 × 39.3 cm

Provenance: Sir P. P. Rubens; N. Lanier; Sir P. Lely; P. Sylvester; ? P. Huart.

1851-2-8-322

Literature: M. Jaffé, *Rubens and Giulio Romano at Mantua,*

49

50

51

52

Art Bulletin, xl, 1958, pp.327f; P. Pouncey and J. A. Gere, *Italian Drawings . . . in the British Museum: Raphael and his Circle,* 1962, under 87.

This is a copy after a drawing by Giulio Romano in the British Museum collection (no.51) which has been very extensively reworked by Rubens.

Giulio Romano (*c.*1499–1546)
51. Perseus disarming, and the origin of coral

Pen and brown ink, with traces of black chalk on blue paper. Some outlines indented. 19.2 × 31.6cm
Provenance: J. Richardson, senior; Malcolm.
1895-9-15-645
Literature: P. Pouncey and J. A. Gere, *Italian Drawings . . . in the British Museum: Raphael and his Circle,* 1962, no.87 (with further bibliographical details).

Allotted by Hartt to the same period as Giulio's studies for the Camerino dei Cesari in the Palazzo Ducale, Mantua, it is an excellent example of the type of mature design by him that Rubens much admired. We may compare it with the weak outline copy of this composition which Rubens has made the basis for what almost amounts to an original drawing of his own (see no.50).

Copy after Annibale Carracci (1560–1609) reworked by Rubens
52. Ignudo with Leda and the Swan

Brush with brown and yellow washes in various shades over black chalk, heightened with white and reworked in grey and brown oil on yellow paper. 55.3 × 40.7cm
Provenance: Sir P. P. Rubens; P. H. Lankrink; J. Richardson, senior; Sir T. Lawrence; S. Woodburn.
London, Victoria and Albert Museum (2307)
Literature: Held, i, p.59; M. Jaffé, *Burlington Magazine,* xcviii, 1956, p.317; Burchard-d'Hulst, 167; J. R. Martin, *The Farnese Gallery,* 1965, p.155.

This is a damaged drawing executed by an anonymous hand in black chalk which has been repaired and extensively reworked by Rubens. It is a copy after part of the ceiling decoration of the Farnese Gallery by Annibale Carracci. Rubens has added a piece of paper in the lower left-hand corner to replace a wedge-shaped part of the drawing that had been torn off. On it, instead of *Apollo and Marsyas* (of which there are traces in the underdrawing above the swan's head), the subject painted on the medallion at this point on the ceiling, Rubens has drawn *Leda and the Swan.* There is no sign of an underdrawing beneath this, which suggests Rubens was himself responsible for repairing the drawing and not the copyist who did the initial drawing in black chalk.

It is very likely that Rubens would have seen the frescoes on the ceiling as early as 1601–2, when he was in Rome working on the altarpiece in Santa Croce in Gerusalemme. He could only have seen the Gallery in its completed form when he was again in Rome from 1606–8 as Annibale had not yet begun his work on the walls during Rubens's first visit.

Studio of Perino del Vaga (1501–47) reworked and retouched by Rubens

53. Part of a basamento for the Last Judgement in the Sistine Chapel,

Pen and brown ink and wash; reworked in brown and grey wash and white bodycolour. The left-hand strip executed by Rubens himself in black chalk, brown wash and white bodycolour; a few touches in yellow bodycolour on both parts of the drawing. 36.5 × 64.1 cm (on the left an 8.5 cm strip has been added by Rubens)

Provenance: Sir P. P. Rubens; Sir T. Lawrence; S. Woodburn; Sir R. Peel; the National Gallery, London; transferred to the British Museum, 1935.

NG.853K (left-hand section) and 853M (right-hand section). 1972 U.792

Literature: H. Voss, *Die Malerei der Spätrenaissance in Rom und Florenz,* 1920, p.74; A. E. Popham, *BMQ,* x, 1935/36 pp.15–17; P. Pouncey and J. A. Gere, *Italian Drawings . . . in the British Museum: Raphael and his Circle,* 1962, no.194.

This was formerly thought to be connected with façade paintings for Rubens's house in Antwerp. Voss first noticed the connection with a frieze in the Palazzo Spada in Rome, which he linked with an unfinished commission of Perino del Vaga for Paul III, which was for a tapestry to go below Michelangelo's *Last Judgement.* This is described by Vasari, and there is a preparatory drawing in the Uffizi, Florence. The drawing, which has been reworked by Rubens, is too weak to be by Perino himself and is no doubt by an assistant. The drawing on the left-hand strip is entirely by Rubens himself. Rubens has made changes to the rest: the legs of the satyrs have been altered; the head of the right-hand figure has been turned into that of an elderly satyr; wings have been added to the eagles' heads; the swag before the left satyr's arm has been enlarged and more fruit has been placed below the satyr's right forearm; the profile mask below the winged woman's left knee has been altered. The drawing originally agreed with the painting in the Palazzo Spada in almost every detail.

Copy after Paolo Veronese (1528–88) reworked by Rubens

54. Christ in the house of Simon the Leper

Brush drawing in brown wash, with grey, brown, yellow and pink bodycolour, heightened with white bodycolour over an underdrawing in black chalk. 52.8 × 91.5 cm

Provenance: Sir P. P. Rubens; Sir J. C. Robinson; Malcolm.

1895-9-15-1053

Literature: Hind, 45.

This is a copy of the painting by Paolo Veronese, *The Feast in the House of Simon the Leper,* now at Turin. It is a drawing of rather poor quality, as we can judge from its upper part. Rubens has reworked the lower part extensively, and has given the figures and faces a Flemish character, as if moving the location of the painting from Venice to Antwerp. Rubens has here taken a drawing of no account and with his brush put life into the figures.

The drawing has been cut above, on the right and at the bottom. The Head of Christ has been drawn on an inset piece of paper.

Domenico Campagnola (c.1500–64) reworked by Rubens

54a. The Assumption of the Virgin

Pen and brown ink, retouched with pen and brown ink and wash, and heightened with white oil-colour. 30.9 × 19.6 cm

Provenance: Sir P. P. Rubens; Sir P. Lely; Malcolm.

1895-9-15-828

The penwork of this drawing is as characteristic of Domenico Campagnola as the reworking is of Rubens. The latter's hand was already noted by Robinson in his catalogue of the Malcolm collection. Like many drawings now attributed to Domenico, this one was formerly thought to be by Titian, no doubt on the strength of a superficial connection with a painting like the Frari *Assumption.* It is not inconceivable that Rubens may have had the drawing in mind when designing his *Virgin of the Holy Innocents* (KdK 197), now in the Louvre.

53

54

54a

59

55

56

57

for his assistants. Rubens was here following the practice of the great masters he had admired in Italy, such as Raphael, who also delegated work to their assistants in this way. While a number of these studies were made in connection with known paintings, many of the finest cannot be related to specific works and may have arisen from the master's fascination with rendering human form and emotion. Stylistically they have a sculptural quality, reflecting Rubens's admiration of Michelangelo, but show less of a renaissance concern for detail than a more unified or baroque representation of the figure in movement. The composition studies of this period are remarkable for Rubens's ability to convey a sense of movement and plastic form with a few strokes of the pen, sometimes elaborated with wash and white bodycolour. The free, masterful touch of these drawings compares very favourably with the more laboured studies of the previous decade.

55. St Amandus and St Walburga

Oil on panel. 66.7 × 24.7 cm
Provenance: Bourgeois bequest, 1811.
Dulwich College Picture Gallery (40)

Study in oil for the reverse of the left-hand wing of the *Raising of the Cross* in Antwerp Cathedral, formerly destined for the high altar of the Church of St Walpurgis in the same city. For the companion study for the right-hand wing, see no.56.

56. St Catherine and St Eligius

Oil on panel. 66.7 × 25.7 cm
Provenance: Bourgeois bequest, 1811.
Dulwich College Picture Gallery (40a)

Study in oil for the reverse of the right-hand wing of the *Raising of the Cross* in Antwerp Cathedral. This painting was commissioned in the summer of 1609 for 2600 guilders for the high altar of St Walpurgis in Antwerp and completed in the summer of the following year. For the companion study for the left-hand wing, see no.55.

57. Study for the figure of Psyche

Black chalk, heightened with white. 57.7 × 40.5 cm
Windsor Castle (6412)
Literature: Glück-Haberditzl, 96; L. van Puyvelde, *Flemish Drawings . . . at Windsor Castle,* no.279; Held, i, p.28; Burchard-d'Hulst, 65.
Inscribed by a later hand in pen, below in the centre, *Del Rubens.*

This is a study from the life for Psyche in a painting of *Cupid and Psyche* in the Stödter collection in Hamburg, according to Burchard-d'Hulst, from the period 1612–15. Held has pointed out that Rubens, following a practice of Michelangelo and Raphael, employed a male nude for this study, and has remarked on how surprisingly few female nude studies Rubens appears to have done.

The Return to Antwerp and the Establishment of the Studio

The decade following Rubens's return to Antwerp from Italy was one of intense activity, including the production of many of his most famous masterpieces. Important commissions for every kind of subject started to flow from the most distinguished quarters, necessitating the systematic organisation of a studio. As assistants or collaborators Rubens recruited painters of outstanding talent to whom he could entrust significant details of composition and execution: Jan 'Velvet' Brueghel (1568–1625), Frans Synders (1579–1657), see no.80, Lucas van Uden (1595–1672/73); and Anthony Van Dyck (1599–1641), who joined the studio in 1620. Rubens also hired skilled engravers to propagate his style, obtaining copyrights at home and abroad to prevent inferior printmakers from reproducing his work. From 1612 he himself became involved in printing as a designer to the Plantin press.

The most common type of drawing we now find is the careful study from the model, generally in black or red chalk, probably intended in many cases as a detailed guide

58r

58v

58. *Recto:* Silenus and Aegle and other figures
Verso: Studies for various compositions

Recto: Pen and brown ink and wash.

Verso: Pen and brown ink with grey wash. 28 × 50.7 cm

Windsor Castle (6417)

Literature: Glück-Haberditzl, 188; L. van Puyvelde,
Flemish Drawings at Windsor Castle, 280; Held, 29;
Burchard-d'Hulst, 51.

The *recto* of this sheet of compositional ideas is largely taken
up with the subject from Virgil of the drunken and
fettered Silenus being crowned by the Naiad, Aegle. Apart
from the renderings of Aegle on the left and in the centre of
the sheet, a third can be made out under the maze of lines in
the upper right-hand corner. Over this one Rubens
appears to have drawn his first idea for the painting of the
Four Continents in Vienna (KdK 111). The pose of Silenus
on the far left recalls that of the sleeping Satyr in the
Bacchanal in the Vienna Academy (KdK 41), which is
generally dated about 1611–12. In the light of such
comparisons Held's dating of the drawing in the years
1611–13 seems highly credible.

The recent uncovering of the *verso* has revealed a
startling array of studies. It is, in fact, very unusual to find
Rubens doing sketches for such diverse subjects on the
same sheet. They all seem to fit well in chronologically
with one another, at any rate, if we may trust what has been
generally assumed about the supposed dates of the related
paintings.

There are three studies of a Dead Christ which can be
linked with Pietà compositions surviving in various
painted versions from the period 1612–14. That in the
Kunsthistorisches Museum, Vienna (515) is signed and
dated 1614. In the upper centre of the sheet is a study of a
horseman with an incomplete repetition below. To the left
is an outline drawing of a horsewoman sitting side-saddle,
holding a hawk. The horseman is closely followed in the
Wolf and Foxhunt in the Metropolitan Museum, New
York. It is probably datable about 1614 or 1615, although
the first recorded mention of a painting of such a subject is
in 1616. The horsewoman was not used as depicted here. In
the New York painting she is placed obscurely on the
extreme right behind the horseman.

In the upper left-hand corner of the sheet is a compositional study for the Beheading of a Female Saint,
whose executioner is a turbaned oriental. A variant for the
beheaded saint is drawn below the composition. Rubens
does not appear to have painted such a picture, but the
conception of the work almost certainly sprung from the
artist's admiration for Elsheimer's paintings. For instance,
Elsheimer's *Martyrdom of St Lawrence* in the National
Gallery, London, has much in common with this sketch.
On the right of the sheet is a study which is a rein-
terpretation of a composition of a group of saints which,
like Rubens's initial ideas for the first *Chiesa Nuova*
altarpiece, is based on Titian (cf. no.26).

59

59. Two studies for St Christopher

Pen and brown ink. 26.7 × 16.6 cm

Provenance: The Rev. C. M. Cracherode.

Gg. 2-231

Literature: Hind, 14; Held, 30; Burchard-D'Hulst, 43.

This is a preliminary idea for the St Christopher on the
outside of the right-hand wing of the Triptych of the
Descent from the Cross of about 1611–14, now in Antwerp
Cathedral (KdK 52). Here Rubens has clearly been influenced by a painting of St Christoper by Adam Elsheimer, of which there are several versions surviving of
uncertain status. One of these, much damaged, is in
Leningrad, and it could conceivably be the original.
Another was engraved by James Heath in 1812, and this
might possibly be identical with a version in the Royal
Collection.

60. Venus grieving over the dead Adonis

Pen and brown ink. 30.5 × 19.8 cm
Provenance: T. J. Bell; L. Burchard.
Washington D.C., National Gallery of Art (B.25,283)
Literature: Held, 23.

The inscription in the artist's hand has been variously read as *Spiritum morientis excipit ore* (or *expectura*, or *exceptans*). The first reading seems to be the most credible and may be translated as 'She revives with the mouth the spirit of the dying [Adonis].' Held has made the plausible suggestion that this drawing was inspired by Rubens's reading of Bion's *Lament for Adonis*. This is an emotional and highly-charged poem, which from the time of the Renaissance was attributed to Bion (*fl.c.*100 BC). This sketch is connected with two other drawings, one of which is in the British Museum collection (no.61). Although executed roughly in pen, rather after the manner of many of Rubens's early drawings, it does reveal in its more fluent penwork the assurance of the mature artist, and is thus very probably from about 1612, the date proposed for the other renderings of this subject. No finished painting appears to have resulted from any of them.

61. Venus lamenting over the dead Adonis
(see colour plate page 104)

Pen and brown ink with brown wash heightened with white. 21.7 × 15.3 cm
Provenance: Paignon-Dijonval; C. G. Vicomte Morel de Vindé; S. Woodburn; Sir T. Lawrence; J. H. Hawkins; Malcolm.
1895-9-15-1064
Literature: Hind, 24 (as by Van Dyck); Held, 22 (as by Rubens); Burchard-d'Hulst, 66.

The composition of this drawing plainly reflects the influence of Correggio, in particular of two of his masterpieces, *Mercury instructing Cupid* and *Jupiter and Antiope,* then in the collection of the Duke of Mantua. Rubens drew at least two other versions of this subject, one now in the National Gallery of Art, Washington D.C. (no.60) and the other in the Print Room at Antwerp. All three drawings were executed about the same period, that is, about 1612, but there is no general agreement as to the order in which the drawings were done. It is quite possible, however, that the present drawing is the earliest of the three, and it is most closely dependent on the antique group of *Menelaus and Patroclus* in the Pitti Palace, Florence, which appears to have been a source of inspiration for the composition.

Guiseppe Niccolo Vicentino (active *c.*1540) after Raphael (1483–1520)
62. Hercules strangling the Nemean Lion

Woodcut. 24.7 × 18.7 cm
Provenance: The Rev. C. M. Cracherode.
1852-6-12-3
Literature: Bartsch, XII, 119. 17. First state.

60

61

63. Hercules strangling the Nemean Lion

Red chalk, brush and red ink, yellow chalk, and touches of black chalk, heightened and corrected with white bodycolour. 31.8×48.4 cm

Provenance: P. J. Mariette; Sir T. Lawrence; Colnaghi, from whom bought by R. S. Clark, 1919. Williamstown, Sterling and Francine Clark Institute
Literature: E. Haverkamp-Begemann and others, *Drawings from the Clark Institute,* 1964, no.20; Burchard-d'Hulst, under 192.

On the strength of a comparison with technically similar drawings Haverkamp-Begemann associates this drawing with others executed in the same way, thought to be from Rubens's Italian period, probably about 1605–8. He considers that in all probability it was drawn within a few years of the artist's return to Antwerp in 1608. For a further discussion of Rubens's treatment of this and other 'Labours of Hercules' see no.184.

A copy of the Williamstown drawing by Antoine Watteau is in the Frits Lugt Collection, Institut Néerlandais, Paris.

62

64. Study for the figure of Christ on the Cross
(see colour plate page 50)
Black chalk heightened with white with some brown wash along the outlines of the right arm. 52.8 × 37 cm
Provenance: R. Payne Knight bequest, 1824.
Oo. 9-26
Literature: Hind, 9; Glück-Haberditzl, 87; Held, 82.

This closely observed study from the life is a mature work of the highest quality, and should be dated about 1614–15, as Held has suggested. This means that it would be later than the preliminary work on the *Raising of the Cross* of about 1609–10 for St Walpurgis, Antwerp. The present drawing cannot be linked specifically with any of the many paintings of Christ on the Cross that later issued from Rubens's studio, nor indeed with any other commission known to us.

65. Mourning figures in a Pietà
Black chalk with black, grey and brown oil colours.
14.1 × 14.2 cm
Provenance: R. Payne Knight bequest, 1824.
Oo.9-19
Literature: Hind, 11.

This is conceivably connected with a detail in a Pietà, but the heads do not occur in any known version of the subject by Rubens. Despite its excellent quality it is possible that the work in black chalk is by an assistant, and that Rubens was only responsible for strengthening it in oils.

64

65

Diuide Filiolo pia diuide basia Mater,
Tempus erit quando basia sletus erunt.

Tu quoque qia saltum secisti matris in aluo
Proavome,pro Christo victima sero cades.

P. Paulus Rubbens intent.

Michel Lasne seulp.

Petrus de Iode excudit

66

67

Michel Lasne (before 1590–1667) after Rubens
66. The Holy Family

Engraving. 26.4 × 17.9 cm
Provenance: C. Fairfax Murray.

1891-4-14-763
Literature: Schneevoogt, 88.123; Rooses, 227 and 1342.

This is one of the few prints engraved by Lasne after a
design by Rubens (see no.67). Lasne worked for him only
in 1617 and 1618.

67. The Holy Family

Pen and brown ink and wash, over black chalk; outlines
traced with the stylus. Diameter 20.1 cm
Provenance: P. J. Mariette; Marquis de Lagoy; Sir
T. Lawrence; S. Woodburn.

1860-6-16-89
Literature: Rooses, 1342; Hind, 6; Held, 142; Burchard-
d'Hulst, 113.

There is little doubt as both Hind and Held have proposed
that despite the difference in shape this is the preparatory
drawing for Michel Lasne's engraving of about 1617–18 of
the *Holy Family* (no.66). There is certainly no other known
circular print surviving with which it can be associated, and
that by Lasne, in reverse, is very close to the drawing in its
details. It is quite likely that the drawing was cut down and
made circular at an early date. The narrow strip of paper
surrounding it was also obviously added at an early date as
Mariette's collector's mark is upon it.

The composition is based on that of a painting, upright
in format, of about 1615, now in the Art Institute of
Chicago (1967.229), with the addition of St Anne leaning
on the back of a cradle in the right foreground in place of
the column lying on its side.

68. A seated lion

Black and yellow chalk and brown wash with on the left
a touch of green watercolour, heightened with white
bodycolour. 28.1 × 42.7 cm
Provenance: R. Payne Knight bequest, 1824.
Oo.9–35
Literature: Hind, 117; Glück-Haberditzl, 98.

A study for the lion seated in the left foreground of the
painting, *Daniel in the lions' den,* which is most probably a
drawing done from the life, unlike *A lioness* (see no.70),
another preliminary study for this painting. The lion
appears once more represented in the same position on a
sheet of summary studies in pen and brown ink in the
Albertina, Vienna. This sheet, however, was done in
Rubens's studio by one of his pupils working from
preliminary drawings, including the present one which
would have been readily available. A study for the lion
standing on a rock to the left of Daniel is in the National
Gallery of Art, Washington, D.C. It is executed in black
chalk, heightened with white, with touches of faded
yellow wash in the background.

69. Study for Daniel in the lions' den

Black chalk, heightened with white bodycolour.
50.7 × 30.2 cm
Provenance: W. Bates; Sir J. C. Robinson; C. Fairfax
Murray.
New York, Pierpont Morgan Library (I.232)
Literature: Glück-Haberditzl, 97; Held, 85; Burchard-
d'Hulst, 110.

A characteristic study, evidently done from the model, for
the figure of Daniel in the painting of *Daniel in the lions' den*
in the National Gallery of Art, Washington D.C. An
indication of the date of this work is suggested by the
painting's appearance in an allegorical painting of *Sight* by
Jan Brueghel in Madrid which is inscribed 1617. Another
painting by the same artist, a *Landscape with Animals,* in
Apsley House, London, includes the central lion and the
lioness on the right of the Washington painting and is dated
1615. Thus we can be reasonably certain that the Washington painting was executed either in 1614 or 1615, and in
any case, we know that it had been executed by early 1618,
as Rubens listed it in his well-known letter of 28 April 1618
among the paintings he was offering to Sir Dudley
Carleton. He describes it as 'Daniel among many lions,
taken from the life. Original, entirely by my own
hand . . .'; however, the quality of the painting in Washington does not seem to support this statement. It seems very
likely that Daniel's pose, cross-legged with hands clasped,
was consciously based by Rubens on the figure of
St Jerome in Cornelis Cort's engraving of the *Penitent
St Jerome* of 1573 after Girolamo Muziano. Rubens's figure
certainly is very closely akin in spirit to Muziano's and it

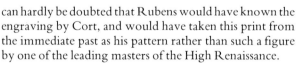

This drawing is a preliminary sketch for the lioness on the right-hand edge of the painting, *Daniel in the lions' den,* formerly in the collection of the Duke of Hamilton and now in the National Gallery of Art, Washington, D.C. It is one of the paintings that Rubens offered to Sir Dudley Carleton, the British Ambassador to the Hague, in a letter dated 28 April 1618, see no. 69. There exists a drawing in Amsterdam in which a lioness is represented as here but in reverse; and this is likely, according to Held, to be connected with a Paduan bronze of a lioness of which Rubens made further studies in pen. Two studies of a crouching lioness in the Victoria and Albert Museum (D.524) were evidently drawn after a bronze during Rubens's years in Italy. Because of the link between the Amsterdam drawing and an Italian bronze it has been suggested that the present drawing, despite its lively vigour, is also not a study after nature. Rubens had a remarkable gift when doing a drawing after an inanimate object of rendering it in a robust life-like manner.

can hardly be doubted that Rubens would have known the engraving by Cort, and would have taken this print from the immediate past as his pattern rather than such a figure by one of the leading masters of the High Renaissance.

70. A lioness (*see colour plate page 103*)
Black and yellow chalk, with grey wash, heightened with white bodycolour. 39.6 × 23.5 cm
Provenance: J. Barnard; Sir T. Lawrence; Sir Robert Peel; National Gallery, London; transferred to the British Museum, 1935.

N.G.853-0, 1973 U.1344
Literature: Rooses, 1428; Glück-Haberditzl, 99; Held, 83.

69

71

71. St Francis kneeling in adoration

Black chalk. 42.2 × 28.6 cm

Provenance: R. Payne Knight bequest.

Oo.9-27

Literature: Hind, 15; H. Vlieghe, *Corpus Rubenianum,* viii, *Saints I,* 1972, no.101a.

Hind rightly pointed out that this is a study connected with the painting in the Liechtenstein collection in Vaduz, *St Francis adoring the crucified Christ* (KdK 170), a typical Counter Reformation representation of this saint. The St Francis in this drawing also bears some relationship to the *St Francis receiving the Stigmata,* a wing from an altarpiece of 1618 in St Gummarus, Lier. Whereas formerly the Liechtenstein painting has been attributed in turn to Rubens and Van Dyck, recently Vlieghe, without giving any explanation, has listed it as the first in a series of copies after a presumed lost original. The whereabouts of a similar study noted by Hind in the possession of Mrs Baird of Colstoun House (Haddington) in 1921, is not known to us. He describes the drawing, however, as showing the saint in a slightly different pose and probably done from the same model.

72

73

72. Hercules victorious over Discord (*see colour plate page 52*)

Red chalk with touches of black chalk. 47.5 × 32 cm
Provenance: J. Barnard; Sir T. Lawrence; S. Woodburn;
J. W. Brett; Henry Vaughan bequest.
1900-8-24-138
Literature: Hind, 22; Glück-Haberditzl, 56; Held, 48;
Burchard-d'Hulst, 188.

Rubens has based this figure of Hercules on his studies of the famous antique statue found in Rome in 1540 and known as the Farnese Hercules. It seems most likely that Rubens derived this Hercules from some sort of copy in his own collection of antiques. Formerly the drawing was thought to be an early work but this view has been abandoned in more recent years, as the drawing can be most convincingly linked with works of the period 1615–22.

The subject of *Hercules victorious over Discord* occurs twice elsewhere in Rubens's work. The first occurrence is in an oil sketch of about 1615–18 in Rotterdam, and in the second, Hercules is on the right of the border of the *Portrait of Charles de Longueval, Count de Bucqot* in Leningrad (KdK 152). From a letter of 19 August 1621 from Robert Schilders to Peiresc we know that this *modello* was executed during July and the first weeks of August 1621. A very similar genius to the one on the left of this drawing is to be found above on the left in *Marie de Médicis as Bellona* of about 1625, in the Louvre (KdK 266, left).

73. Study for Mary Magdalene (*see colour plate page 102*)

Black chalk, heightened with white chalk.
33.5 × 24.3 cm
Provenance: P. Crozat; Sir T. Lawrence; J. P. Heseltine, by whom presented to the British Museum.
1912-12-14-5
Literature: Hind, 16.

This study, apparently done from the life, was clearly drawn with a painting of the Penitent Magdalene in mind. But, as with several other drawings of this type, no known commission can be connected directly with the kneeling nude figure. Some general similarities are to be found in the suppliant female figure bending before Christ in the *Christ and the Penitents* in Munich (KdK 176), a painting of about 1618. But the pose is not sufficiently close for one to be able to assume that Rubens had this drawing particularly in mind when he designed this composition. There is an even more tenuous link with the sensuous kneeling Magdalene, who wipes Christ's feet with her hair in the painting now in Leningrad, *Christ in the house of Simon the Pharisee* (KdK 179).

74

74. Study for one of the weeping women

Black chalk heightened with white chalk. 26.3 × 21.6 cm
Provenance: William Fawkener bequest.

5212-63

Literature: Hind, 10.

Although Hind suggested that this might possibly be an offset of a drawing, it is much more likely that its present appearance is due to rubbing. This latter possibility is more probable because some of the strokes of chalk are much stronger than others. This drawing, like several others of the same type, cannot be linked specifically with a weeping woman in any of the known surviving *Pietàs*. Its date is not easy to determine but it could conceivably be from the period 1615–20.

75

76r

76v

75. Two Franciscans

Black and white chalk with some red chalk on the faces.
56 × 40.3 cm
Chatsworth, Devonshire Collection (964a)
Literature: Glück-Haberditzl, 113; Held, 93; H. Vlieghe,
Corpus Rubenianum, viii, *Saints I,* 1972, no.102c.

These are two studies after the model for the *Last Communion of St Francis* of 1619 in Antwerp (KdK 190). This masterly painting, executed throughout by the artist, was commissioned by Jasper Charles for the Altar of St Francis in the Church of the Recollects in Antwerp. The Franciscan with his arms outstretched is a study for the friar holding the Saint, who is about to receive communion. In the painting this Franciscan is shown bending rather more forward than in the drawing. The lower part of the back of his habit has been drawn by Rubens between the two figures. The lower study of a Franciscan with a cowl over his head is to be found in the background of the painting on the right-hand edge.

There are two further studies of Franciscans at Amsterdam and in the collection of Count Antoine Seilern. A preliminary rapid sketch in pen and ink, a first idea for the painting, is in the Cabinet des Estampes, Antwerp. Another rapid sketch in chalk, this time giving the general scheme of the composition, is in an English private collection (no.84). It is of special interest because of an inscription in the artist's hand from which it is clear with what care Rubens planned the interior lighting of his pictures.

76. *Recto:* A seated woman
Verso: Studies of a baby

Black chalk touched with white chalk. 40.9 × 28.5 cm
Provenance: A. Geddes; S. Woodburn.
1933-4-11-1
Literature: Hind, *BMQ,* viii, 1933, p.1.

The sketches on both sides of this sheet are clearly studies from the life. Neither of them, however, can be connected with any particular commission. But it is just possible that the drawing on the *recto* was a first idea for the shawled figure of Martha in the background of the *Penitent Magdalene* of 1612–15, now in Vienna. Although the style of the drawing would not be at variance with such a hypothesis, usually such drawings after the model were closely followed in the related composition.

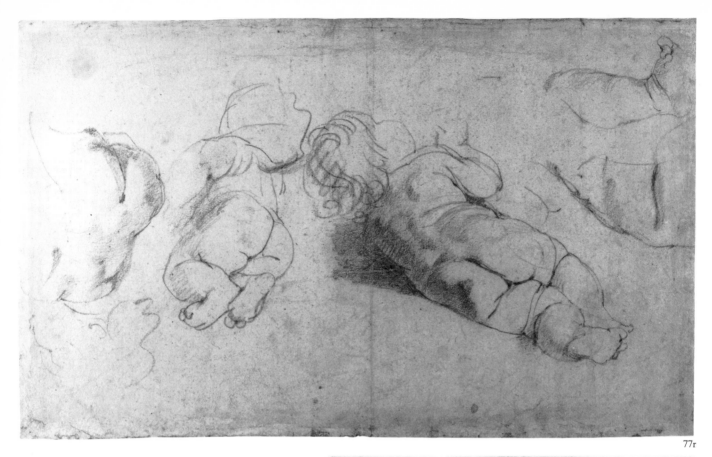

77r

77. *Recto* and *Verso*, Studies of a child

Black chalk. 30.2 × 50.8 cm

Provenance: Samuel Rogers and thence by descent to his great-niece Miss Julia Sharpe; presented by the executors of the late Miss Julia Sharpe.

1946-4-13-191

Literature: L. Burchard, 'Studies of a naked infant by Peter Paul Rubens', in *Schaeffer Galleries Bulletin*, no.3, New York, December 1947.

On both sides of this sheet the artist has sketched from the life charming studies of a child about two years old who lies asleep naked and uncovered on a bed. This must be an instance of the artist seizing an opportunity to make these delightful records of oblivious and totally relaxed infancy. All the same it is clear from this sheet that the child did not lie still in its sleep. The studies on the *recto* of the present drawing were subsequently used as models for some of the children in the painting in the Louvre *The Virgin of the Holy Innocents* of about 1618–20 (KdK 197). Further, more complete studies of a child, also in black chalk, were made on a sheet now in the Louvre (inv. no. R.F.29943).

The studies on the *verso* of the British Museum drawing do not appear to have been used afterwards by Rubens in any of his paintings.

77v

79

79. A shepherd walking to the left

Watercolour washes and bodycolour over an underdrawing in black chalk. 28.7 × 18.9 cm

Mrs Eliot Hodgkin

Literature: Burchard-d'Hulst, 90.

A study for one of the shepherds in the *Adoration of the Shepherds,* in Marseilles, and one of the predella panels from the altarpiece of the *Adoration of the Magi* in St John's Church at Malines, work on which was begun before 23 January, 1619. This shepherd is reminiscent of one in Titian's woodcut of the *Adoration of the Magi,* but he is not shown here taking off his cap as in the print. The shepherd in the present drawing occurs again in a preparatory drawing, now in the Louvre, corrected by Rubens for an engraving of the *Adoration of the Shepherds* of 1620 by Lucas Vosterman.

This shepherd, although with his head somewhat turned, is also present in the *modello* for an *Adoration of the Shepherds* in Edinburgh. Besides this figure the *modello* includes others drawn from various Rubens paintings, especially the *Adoration of the Shepherds* in Munich. A larger version of this subject deriving from the Edinburgh *modello* does not appear to have survived.

78

78. Portrait of Hendrik van Thulden

Black chalk. 37.4 × 26.2 cm

Provenance: J. Richardson, senior; T. Hudson; Sir Joshua Reynolds.

1845-12-8-5

Literature: Hind, 44 (as by Van Dyck); Held, 86; Burchard-d'Hulst, 109.

This is a costume-study for the portrait in Munich, with the sitter in the academic dress of a bachelor of theology. Originally the head of the sitter was sunk more deeply into the collar. The head has been raised so that there are two pairs of eyes visible. In the painting Rubens omitted the biretta. Another portrait of van Thulden by Rubens which shows him kneeling before a crucifix formerly hung over his tomb. He was pastor at St Joris, Antwerp, from 1613 to his death in 1617.

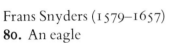

80

81r

81v

Frans Snyders (1579–1657)

80. An eagle

Pen and brown ink and wash. 28.1 × 20.3 cm

Provenance: J. van Haecken; Phillipps-Fenwick; presented anonymously.

1946-7-13-176

This sketch is a preliminary study for the eagle in the painting by Rubens, *Prometheus bound,* in the Philadelphia Museum of Art, painted in the period 1612–18. Sometimes the assistance in the studio was so far devolved that the responsibility for providing a design for an important feature fell on the shoulders of another. In the case of the Philadelphia painting, Frans Snyders not only painted the eagle but drew the present drawing, so characteristic of him in its strident penwork. The figure of Prometheus is here barely indicated by a few strokes of black chalk.

82

81. *Recto:* Portrait of Pieter van Hecke
Verso: Two studies for a 'St Cecilia'

Black chalk. 41.3 × 34.5 cm

Provenance: J. Richardson, senior; T. Hudson; J. Thane;
R. Cosway; W. Russell.

1885-5-9-48

Literature: Hind, 91.

The drawing on the *recto* is a preparatory study for the
portrait-painting of Pieter van Hecke formerly in the
collection of Edmond de Rothschild, Paris. The sitter was
the husband of Clara Fourment, the artist's sister-in-law.
Despite the attribution of this portrait by many scholars to
Van Dyck, there is no doubt that the present drawing is by
Rubens. This is given corroboration by the fact that the
studies on the *verso* are connected with Rubens's painting
of *St Cecilia* in Berlin (KdK 435).

82. Two studies of a river god

Black chalk squared in black chalk. 41.4 × 24 cm

Provenance: Howard Wicklow; F.T.P.; Henry Adams;
Mrs Henry P. Quincy.

Boston Museum of Fine Arts (20.813)

Literature: Held, 33; J. R. Martin, *Corpus Rubenianum*,
xvi, *The Decorations for the Pompa Introitus Ferdinandi*,
1972, p.198, no.50b.

As Held has pointed out, these studies cannot be precisely
linked with any of Rubens's works, although similar
figures occur in works of the 1620s. One of these is the river
god in the drawing of the *Vestal Tuccia* in the Louvre,
which M. Jaffé has specifically linked with the Boston
drawing. The *Vestal Tuccia* can probably be dated about
1622 as there is a rapidly executed reference sketch on the
verso for one scene of the Médicis cycle, *Louis XIII comes of
age*.

Ludwig Burchard, however, thought the present sketch
was for the river god, Marañon, on the Arch of the Mint
(Archus Monetalis), part of the decorations for the triumphal entry of the Cardinal-Infante Ferdinand into
Antwerp. From a comparison of Rubens's oil-sketch for
this Arch, now in the Antwerp Museum, with van
Thulden's etching, which records the final arrangement,
we know this river god was moved from the front face of
the Arch to its rear-side. But neither on the oil-sketch nor
on the etching does the river god appear in the same
direction as in the drawing and furthermore the figure of
Marañon has noticeable differences in his pose to that of the
river gods in the Boston drawing. Because of this and
because of the difference in lighting between the sketch and
the drawing Martin is inclined to reject Burchard's
proposed linking of the Boston drawing with the Arch of
the Mint decoration. His most decisive argument against
this is, however, that the style of the drawing suggests that
it was done considerably earlier in date than 1635, the year
of the Entry. The early 1620s seem altogether a much more
likely time for its execution.

83. Rape of the Sabine women

Pen and brown ink with black chalk. 10 × 25 cm
England, Private Collection

In this spirited sketch, probably from the period 1610–14,
Rubens undoubtedly received his initial inspiration from
Raphael's design for the *Massacre of the Innocents,* engraved
by Marcantonio Raimondi (Bartsch, xiv, 19.18). But quite
apart from the differences necessitated by the change of
subject he has reinterpreted Raphael in a thoroughly
individual fashion. We meet this very free form of
indebtedness again, this time to Michelangelo, in another
drawing very close in style and date to the present one. This
is the fragmentary study, now in a private collection in
Holland, for a *Fall of the Damned,* which certainly antedates
the artist's own painting of the subject.

84. *Recto:* The last communion of St Francis of Assisi
Verso: The discovery of Callisto's shame

Recto: Red and black chalk. *Verso:* Red chalk, heightened
with white bodycolour, and partly pen and brown ink.
28.5 × 23.5 cm
Provenance: acquired on the London Art Market, 1931.
England, Private Collection
Literature: Burchard-d'Hulst, 122; H. Vlieghe, *Corpus
Rubenianum,* viii, *Saints I,* 1972, no.102b.

In this rough sketch for the composition of the altarpiece,
The last communion of St Francis, at Antwerp (KdK 190),
Rubens gives the merest hint of the main features of the
painting including the architectural setting of the composition. This is one of the small number of such rough
drafted compositions by him to have survived. In a note in
Italian Rubens has settled how he will manage the lighting
of the subject: 'The whole group [of Franciscans] in
shadow and a resonant light from the sun sufficient
through the window'. This commission, paid for on 17
May 1619, was one over which Rubens took particular
trouble, as he appears to have executed much of the
painting himself. There is also another rapid sketch in pen,
now in the Antwerp Print Room, in which he roughly

indicates the general position of the various figures in the composition; however, neither in the present drawing nor in that at Antwerp does Rubens show the priest giving communion as in the painting. In both sketches the Host is on the point of being offered, whereas in the painting it is held up before the Saint. This important change that Rubens effects in the final work made possible the upward gaze of St Francis which is the dramatic focal point of the whole composition.

On the *verso* is a rapid sketch of nymphs disrobing Callisto, probably also dating from about 1620, and undoubtedly inspired by the similar group of figures on the left of Titian's famous painting of the same subject, belonging to the Duke of Sutherland. The sheet has been cut down on all sides, so the right-hand part of the composition with Diana is missing; however, there is below a small study in pen and ink of Diana and a nymph drying the goddess's feet, a motif which Rubens has borrowed from Titian's companion painting of *Diana and Actaeon*.

85. Rome Triumphant

Red chalk, with slight touches of brown wash, heightened with white bodycolour. 38 × 42.9 cm
Provenance: ?W. Roscoe; Sir T. Lawrence;
Sir J. C. Robinson; Malcolm.
1895-9-15-1051
Literature: Rooses, 1468; Hind, 29; Held, under 49.

This drawing is probably a variant rendering of the design of *Roma Triumphans,* one of the series of the *History of Constantine,* destined to be turned into tapestries, commissioned by Louis XIII during the artist's first stay in Paris in January and February 1622. The initial ideas for this and related Roman themes, such as the earlier cycle of Decius Mus, were spread in profusion on a sheet at Berlin (inv. no. 4249) and from this emerged in much simplified form, in a pen and wash drawing in the Albertina, the main outlines of the composition, which Rubens then elaborated in the oil-sketch, now in the Mauritshuis at the Hague (KdK 233).

84v

85

The 'Lion hunt' and the 'Fall of the Damned'

In a letter of September 13 1621, referring to a commission for Sir John Digby, English ambassador to Brussels, Rubens wrote: 'I have almost finished a large picture, entirely by my hand and in my opinion one of my best, representing a Hunt of Lions, the figures as large as life.' This celebrated painting, now at Munich, was the culmination of a number of hunting scenes painted by Rubens during the previous five or six years. The earlier *Lion hunt* at Dresden preceded a series of hunting scenes, including a (now destroyed) *Lion hunt,* commissioned by Maximilian, Elector of Bavaria, and painted *c.*1615–16. Far from merely repeating these, the painting at Munich is a fresh approach to the subject, more successfully combining complex movement and violent action into a unified composition. The National Gallery oil-sketch (no.88), Rubens's first surviving treatment of the theme, has its roots in the master's early attempts to render violence, such as in the *Battle of the Amazons* (no.21), strongly influenced by Leonardo's *Battle of the Standard* (cf.nos.22–23). The other

oil-sketch on display (no.86), like the drawing (no.87), is related to the Munich painting, but the *verso* shows that Rubens began to plan his most demanding commission, the Médicis cycle (see nos.151–53) at about this time. The large sheet (no.89) contains sketches for the *Lion hunt* and the *Fall of the Damned,* also at Munich, another of his most turbulent works on which he was apparently working simultaneously. Rubens's own satisfaction with this composition is evident from the series of drawings based on it (nos.90–94), apparently done by an assistant under the artist's direct supervision. The more finished of them have been substantially reworked by Rubens himself.

86v

86. *Recto:* A lion hunt
Verso: Marriage of Marie de Médicis

Oil on panel. 54 × 44 cm

Provenance: acquired by the then Lord Cholmondeley in 1751 and thence by descent to the present owner.

The Marquess of Cholmondeley

Literature: Puyvelde, *Esquisses,* pl.17; Wildenstein, 1950, no.20.

This is a sketch for the *Lion hunt* in Munich (KdK 154). Burchard convincingly dated the sketches on both sides of the panel to about 1622. The sketch on the *verso* was painted for the large canvas in the Médicis cycle (KdK 247) which was executed in 1622–3. An oil-sketch closer to the final painting is in Munich.

Three studies in black chalk for details in the *Lion hunt* are known. One for the falling rider is in the British Museum collection (no.87), and the other of the swordsman on horseback on the left of the composition is in an English private collection. This study had been already used and followed in a previous commission, the *Lion hunt* of about 1616, known to us from the fine replica formerly in the Spencer-Churchill collection (see no.89). In this the swordsman is an Oriental just as in the drawing, whereas in the later work he has become a European. The third study for the horseman on the right, *An Oriental thrusting with a lance* (Held 96) is now at Berlin (Inv. no. 26383).

87. A man falling from a horse: Study of the left hand of the falling man

Black chalk. 32.4 × 30.7 cm

Provenance: P. H. Lankrink; R. Payne Knight bequest, 1824.

Oo. 9–18

Literature: Hind, 12; Glück-Haberditzl, 91; Held, 97.

This is one of the finest studies from the model which Rubens drew in connection with his hunting and battle pictures. The study on the separate piece of paper in the upper left-hand corner is for the left hand of the falling man. He occurs not only in the *Lion hunt* of about 1622 at Munich (KdK 154) and in the oil-sketch for it in the collection of the Marquess of Cholmondeley (see no.86), but also in the sketch for the *Conquest of Tunis by Charles V* (KdK 401) of about 1620, at Berlin.

87

88. A Lion hunt

Oil on panel. 74 × 105.7 cm

Provenance: J. E. van Jabach; by descent to the von Merwig family; Sir R. Peel.

London, National Gallery (853P)

Literature: G. Martin, *National Gallery Catalogues: The Flemish School, c. 1600–c. 1900,* 1970, pp.182–7.

This sketch belongs to a group of preliminary studies on panel on which the artist continued to work towards a solution of the problems relating to the composition in hand. In the case of the present sketch, for instance, Rubens is still in the process of settling the ideas which finally bear fruit in the Dresden *Lion hunt* (KdK 113), and the *Lion and tiger hunt* at Rennes, which both can be dated reasonably about 1615–17. His usual practice was to fix the details of his compositions in preliminary drawings before beginning to paint his oil-sketch. Here, however, in this rapidly executed sketch in grisaille, full of life and vigour, Rubens is still in the midst of determining the central motif of the composition, that is, the lion attacking a huntsman from the rear. In the upper right-hand corner of the panel Rubens has done a small preliminary rapid drawing with the brush as a 'try-out' for this tricky detail. Then he proceeded to elaborate this on a larger scale as an integral part of the composition. In so doing he has imparted to the lion's body the muscular tension (essential to a life-like representation) of an animal that has just sprung upon its prey.

89. *Recto:* Large sheet of studies, with below, a large dragon and struggling figures, and above, two studies for a lion hunt

Verso: Studies of figures being borne up by angels

Pen and brown ink. 57.4 × 48.5 cm

Provenance: P. H. Lankrink; Sir J. Reynolds; ? Sir T. Lawrence; P. L. Huart; W. Russell.

1885-5-9-51

Literature: Hind, 1; D. Rosand, *Art Bulletin,* li, 1969, p.31f.

The dragon and the mass of animals and men on the lower half of the *recto* were drawn in preparation for the lowest part of the *Fall of the Damned* in Munich (KdK 194). Some have mistakenly assumed that this part of the painting was executed by an assistant, a proposal to which an examination of the original, in our view, lends no support.

On the upper part of the sheet, and now appearing upside down because the paper was originally folded, are two sketches for a *Lion hunt*. In its composition it is most closely related to a *Lion hunt* belonging to a series of hunting scenes, probably painted about 1615–16 for the Elector of Bavaria. Although the original of this was destroyed in a fire in Bordeaux, we can to some extent gauge its appearance from the best surviving studio replica, that formerly in the collection of Captain E. G. Spencer-Churchill. It seems very likely that this is the painting listed by Rubens in his letter to Sir Dudley Carleton of 28 April 1618: 'Hunt of Men on Horseback and Lions begun by one

89r

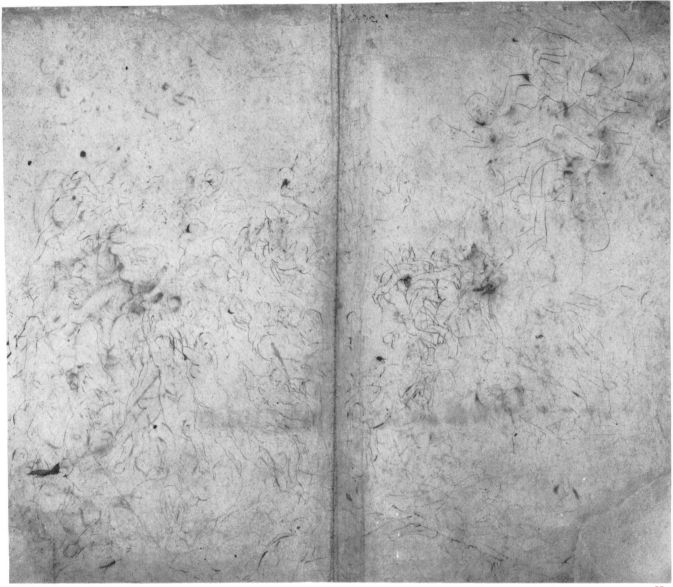

of my pupils, after the one that I made for his Most Serene Highness of Bavaria, but all retouched by my hand'.

It is very likely that all these studies were drawn at the same date, 1621, the year when according to the artist's nephew, the *Fall of the Damned* was painted. The sketches for a *Lion hunt* appear to derive from the Elector of Bavaria's painting; however, Rubens could be reinterpreting the composition afresh for use in the *Fall of the Damned*.

The delicate and somewhat faint drawings on the *verso* are for the *Assumption of the Blessed,* a painting now in Munich and, it seems, executed entirely by assistants in Rubens's studio.

90–94. Five drawings connected with the 'Fall of the Damned' *(see colour plate of 94 on page 49)*

90. Initial drawing in black chalk with light brown wash, worked up with brush and oil colour. 70.7 × 48 cm

Provenance: P. H. Lankrink; Sir J. Thornhill; Sir B. West; probably Sir T. Lawrence; S. Woodburn; Sir R. Peel; the National Gallery, London; transferred to the British Museum, 1935.

N.G.853–A

Literature: Rooses, 1413; A. E. Popham, *BMQ*, x, 1935, pp.10–12; J. Müller-Hofstede, *Wallraf-Richartz Jahrbuch*, xxvii, 1965, p.319.

91. Black and red chalk with wash in various shades of brown. 74.8 × 47.6 cm

Provenance: The same as above.

N.G.853–B

Literature: Rooses, 1415; A. E. Popham, *op. cit.,* pp.10–12; J. Müller-Hofstede, *op.cit.,* p.325.

90

92

91

92. Initial drawing in black chalk with brown wash worked up with brush and oil colour. 75 × 47.8 cm

Provenance: The same as above.

N.G.853–C

Literature: Rooses 1412; A. E. Popham, *op. cit.,* pp.10–12; J. Müller-Hofstede, *op. cit.,* p.325.

93. Black and red chalk with watercolour washes and bodycolour. 72.3 × 47 cm

Provenance: The same as above.

N.G.853–D

Literature: Rooses, 1414; A. E. Popham, *op.cit.,* pp.10–12; J. Müller-Hofstede, *op.cit.,* 325–6.

94. Initial drawing in black and red chalk, with grey wash, worked up with brush and oil colour. 71 × 47.5 cm

Provenance: E. Jabach; P. Crozat; R. Payne Knight bequest, 1824.

Oo.3–9

Literature: Rooses, 1416; Hind, 2; J. Müller-Hofstede, *op.cit.,* pp.326–30.

These five drawings, although they are not of equally excellent quality, should be considered as a group, because they evidently formed part of the same commission or were executed with the same end in view. The fact that they have not all been worked up to the same degree of finish has created a false division between the flat and uninteresting appearance of those which have not been enlivened by being worked up in oil, and those which have so benefited. In our view, Popham is right in proposing that the work with the brush was probably done by Rubens himself. The painting in oil on these drawings is certainly most impressive and thoroughly worthy of the master.

The initial drawing, however, is not by Rubens, and there is strong internal evidence to suggest that these drawings, so far from being of a preparatory nature, were all, in fact, executed after the painting in Munich (KdK 194). Quite apart from the way in which the groups of falling figures are arranged to fill the sheets of more or less uniform size, and the avoidance of overlapping of the different groups of figures, there is an additional and decisive point to be noted. In the one instance where the string of falling figures is still incomplete at the bottom of the sheet (see no.90), Rubens has changed the critical figure, i.e. the lowest of the figures falling on the left, from a damned man who clings desperately to the hair of a woman falling headlong, to a winged devil. This new figure has been freely sketched in with the brush, with

94

some pentimenti of the limbs, but without any supporting initial drawing underneath. This lack of an underdrawing would appear to give further support to the idea that the preliminary work is not by Rubens but that of an assistant. If one compares this point in the drawing with the same point in the finished painting, we find that the falling man who has been replaced by a winged devil is himself seated on other falling figures, which constitute in the painting the lower limit of this string of figures. This is a clear indication that these drawings, which can reasonably be considered as a group, were executed after the painting and not beforehand.

It is not, however, immediately apparent for what purpose they could have been intended. It may be that they were meant to serve as preparatory drawings for five separate engravings. But as no such engravings were apparently carried out, their use in Rubens's studio must remain a matter for speculation.

Drawings after the Antique

The earliest known copies of antique art by Rubens date from his stay in Italy. There, alongside his study of Italian Renaissance paintings, he copied the famous statues in Rome, including the Laocoön, the Apollo Belvedere, the Belvedere torso, the Hermaphrodite and many others (see nos.13,14,18,19 and 20). Antique friezes and monumental sculpture profoundly influenced Rubens's own compositions, but his interest apparently embraced almost every relic of the ancient world. In 1618 his admiration led him to acquire the collection of antiquities formed by Sir Dudley Carleton, English ambassador to The Hague. Rubens copied several works from this collection. The majority of those on display, however, are after small coins, medals, or cameos and drawn in pen and ink, ready to be engraved. A planned edition of antique cameos was apparently abandoned (see no.95) and it has been suggested that a similar publication of coins was projected. Whether this would have included Rubens's copies of imitation antique coins by the Italian medallist Valerio Belli (1468–1546) is a matter for speculation.

95. The Triumph of Licinius

Pen and brown ink. 19 × 25 cm

Provenance: G. E. Bullen.

1919-11-11-22

Literature: Rooses, 1223; Hind, 53; H. M. van der Meulen-Schregardus, *Petrvs Pavlvs Rvbens Antiquarivs,* 1975, G.70a.

This is a much enlarged copy of the cameo of the Triumph of Licinius in the Cabinet des Médailles, Paris. The size of the cameo is indicated in the lower left-hand corner by an outline sketch inscribed *grandezza della Pietra.* Since 1621 Rubens and his antiquarian friend Pieresc had been planning a publication of the better-known antique gems. It appears that only eight engravings of gems and the title page, *Varie figueri de Agati Antique desiniati de Peetro Paulo Rubbenie Grave Par Lucas Vostermans c. Paulus Pontius* were executed. This drawing is a design for one of this series and it seems most likely that Vorsterman rather than Pontius is responsible for the engraving (see no.96).

Attributed to Lucas Vorsterman I (1595–1675)
96. The Triumph of Licinius

Engraving.18.4 × 22.6 cm

1919-11-11-23

Literature: Rooses, 1223.

Rubens in a letter to Valavez of 3 July 1625 described this print as the 'Triumphant Quadriga, very fine and worthy of consideration'. The artist hopes that Signor Girolamo Aleandro will be able to interpret the subject and identify the Emperor. The antiquity of this cameo is now doubted and it is thought to be a work of the sixteenth century.

95

96

97

97. Profile of a woman

Pen and light brown ink. 6.7 × 2.5 cm

Provenance: Sir P. Lely.

1854-6-28-106

This tiny fragment probably drawn after the Antique was formerly attributed to Perino del Vaga. It was recognised to be by Rubens by A. E. Popham in 1937.

Thirty heads after antique coins, etc.

Thirty heads on twenty-eight pieces of paper, probably cut down from larger sheets.

They were engraved by Gerard van der Gucht under the title, *Antique Greek and Roman Coins, Gems, etc. Engraved from Original Drawings of Rubens by G. Van der Gucht,* published 30 May 1740.

Provenance: P. H. Lankrink; J. Richardson, senior.

Literature: Van der Gucht, 1–30; Rooses, 1404; Hind, 55–82.

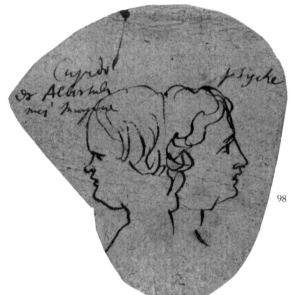

98

98. Twin heads of cupid and Psyche

Pen and brown ink. Irregularly cut, maximum height and width 7.9 × 7.5 cm

1858-6-26-134

Literature: Van der Gucht, 1; Hind, 55; Glück-Haberditzl, 81.

The Latin inscription on the left in the artist's hand indicates the cupid's features are those of his son Albert who had been born in 1614. The drawing may be reasonably dated 1615.

99. Twin heads of Silenus and a satyr

Pen and brown ink. 11 × 12.7 cm

1858-6-26-135

Literature: Van der Gucht, 2; Hind 56; Glück-Haberditzl, 82.

The Latin inscription in the artist's hand refers to possible mediums that might be used in the application of the design, 'The one might be of ivory, the other . . .'.

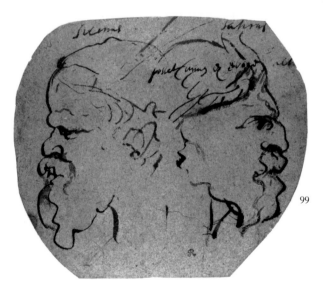

99

100

100. Thales

Pen and brown ink. 5.7 × 4 cm

1858-6-26-137

Literature: Van der Gucht, 4; Hind, 58.

This profile head is based on a model by Valerio Belli (1468–1546), of which there is an example in lead in the British Museum.

101. Hermatene

Pen and brown ink. 15.2 × 17.5 cm

1858-6-26-136

Literature: Van der Gucht, 3; Rooses, 1404 and 1364; Hind, 57; Glück-Haberditzl, 83.

The Latin inscription on the helmet 'of iron, or ebony, or electrum' and on the heads, 'of ivory' could well refer to some use that Rubens was contemplating for the design. The inscription in the lower right-hand corner presumably refers to another design that has been cut off.

101

102. Bias

Pen and brown ink. 6.4 × 7.7 cm

1858-6-26-138

Literature: Van der Gucht, 6 & 5; Hind, 59.

These two heads are based on a medal by Valerio Belli of which there is an example in lead in the British Museum.

102

103

103. Epaminondas

Pen and brown ink. 5.2 × 4.2 cm

1858-6-26-139

Literature: Van der Gucht, 8; Hind, 61.

This profile head is based on a medal by Valerio Belli, of which an example in lead is in the British Museum.

104. Lysander and Solon

Pen and brown ink. 5.8 × 7.6 cm

1858-6-26-140

Literature: Van der Gucht, 9 & 7; Hind, 60.

104

The profile head on the left of Lysander is based on a medal by Valerio Belli and that on the right of Solon is also derived from one by the same Italian medallist. There is an example of the former in silver (see no.108) and of the latter in lead in the British Museum.

105. Hercules

Pen and brown ink. 5.6 × 4.8 cm

1858-6-26-141

Literature: Van der Gucht, 10; Hind, 62.

This is possibly an adaptation from an Italian Renaissance medal of the sixteenth century, such as that exhibited for comparison (see no.106), or more probably is based on a piece of sculpture.

105

Anonymous artist, Italian, 16th century

106. Hercules

Cast in bronze. 4.1 cm

Provenance: Bank of England.

British Museum, Department of Coins and Medals

1865-3-24-2339

106

108

109

107. Lysander
Pen and brown ink. 8 × 5.5 cm
1858-6-26-141★
Literature: Van der Gucht, 11; Hind, 63.

Valerio Belli (1468–1564)
108. Lysander
Medal, struck in silver. 2.9 cm
Provenance: Parkes Weber gift.
British Museum, Department of Coins and Medals
1906-11-3-996

From Belli's series of portraits of the great figures of antiquity. Though not produced with intent to deceive they were often believed by later collectors to be ancient.

109. Epaminondas
Pen and brown ink. 8.5 × 6.2 cm
1858-6-26-142
Literature: Van der Gucht, 12; Hind, 64.

A larger copy (cf. no.103 for a smaller one) after a medal by Valerio Belli.

110

112

111

114

113

110. Democritus?

Pen and brown ink. 7.4 × 6.4 cm

1858-6-26-143

Literature: Van der Gucht, 13; Hind, 65.

Evidently, as the inscription *In Grande* ('In the large') seems to imply, this is drawn after a large sculpture. Hind has rightly pointed out on the basis of Lucas Vosterman's engraving after a classical bust of Democritus, that this drawing is more likely to be of him than Socrates, who was Van der Gucht's identification.

111. Marius

Pen and brown ink. 6.2 × 5.8 cm

1858-6-26-144

Literature: Van der Gucht, 14; Hind, 66.

This profile head is based on a medal by Valerio Belli of which there is an example in lead in the British Museum (no.112). The first part of the inscription on this drawing is the completion of the second word on the drawing of Lysander and Solon (no.104).

Valerio Belli (1468–1564)

112. Marius

Cast in lead. 3 cm

British Museum, Department of Coins and Medals
M0099

From Belli's series of portraits of the great figures of antiquity.

113. Cato the Elder

Pen and brown ink. 6.4 × 5.4 cm

1858-6-26-145

Literature: Van der Gucht, 15; Hind 67.

This profile head is based on a medal by Valerio Belli of which an example in lead is in the British Museum (no.114).

Valerio Belli (1468–1564)

114. Cato the Elder

Cast in lead. 2.85 cm

Provenance: Carlyon Britton gift.

British Museum, Department of Coins and Medals
1924-8-12-2

From Belli's series of portraits of the great figures of antiquity.

115

116

115. Caligula

Pen and brown ink. 4.5 × 3.2 cm

1858-6-26-148

Literature: Van der Gucht, 18; Hind, 70.

Hind rejected Julius Caesar, Van der Gucht's title, in favour of Claudius; however, to judge from a comparison with the coins, Caligula appears to be the correct identification (see no.116).

116. Aureus of Caligula

Coin struck at Rome or Lyon in AD 37–8. 2 cm

Provenance: C. M. Cracherode gift, 1799.

British Museum, Department of Coins and Medals
BMC Cal.14

117. 'Seneca': full-face

Pen and brown ink. Oval. 5 × 4.4 cm

1858-6-26-147

Literature: Van der Gucht, 17; Hind 69.

As with the following drawing (no.118) this is based on an antique bust that was in Rubens's own collection.

118. 'Seneca': a profile. Part of the head of a bearded man

Pen and brown ink over an underdrawing in black chalk. Diameter 10.9 cm

1858-6-26-146

Literature: Van der Gucht, 16; Hind, 68.

This and a drawing of '*Seneca': full-face* (no.117) are based on an antique bust that was in Rubens's own collection. It was one of many surviving copies which were taken to be of the Roman philosopher and dramatist Seneca until an inscribed bust with differing features was found at Rome in 1813.

119. Augustus

Pen and brown ink. 4.5 × 3.2 cm

1858-6-26-149

Literature: Van der Gucht, 19; Hind, 71.

Rubens has clearly copied this from a commemorative coin of Augustus Divus, struck under Tiberius (see no.120).

120. As of the deified Emperor Augustus

Coin struck at Rome during the reign of his successor Tiberius, *c.* AD 20–30.

British Museum, Department of Coins and Medals
BMC Tib.149

The Emperor is shown wearing a radiate crown to denote his divinity.

117

118

120

119

121

121. Tiberius

Pen and brown ink. 5.4 × 3.7 cm
1858-6-26-150
Literature: Van der Gucht, 20; Hind, 72.

122. Caligula

Pen and brown ink. 5 × 2.9 cm
1858-6-26-151
Literature: Van der Gucht, 21; Hind, 73.

122

123. Augustus

Pen and brown ink. 5.2 × 3.5 cm
1858-6-26-152
Literature: Van der Gucht, 22; Hind, 74.

Copied from an antique coin, such as that exhibited for comparison (see no.124).

124. Dupondius of the deified Emperor Augustus

Coin struck at Rome during the reign of Claudius (AD 41–54). 3.2 cm
British Museum, Department of Coins and Medals
BMC Claud. 224

Augustus is shown with a radiate crown. This coin may have been issued in AD 42, to mark the deification of Augustus's wife Livia, who appears on the reverse.

123

124

125. Nero

Pen and brown ink. 5.3 × 3.9 cm

1858-6-26-153

Literature: Van der Gucht, 23; Hind, 75.

Copied from an antique coin such as the sestertius exhibited for comparison (see no. 129).

126. Galba

Pen and brown ink. 6.5 × 4.8 cm

1858-6-26-154

Literature: Van der Gucht, 24; Hind, 76.

127. Otho

Pen and brown ink. 5.4 × 3.8 cm

1858-6-26-155

Literature: Van der Gucht, 25; Hind, 77.

128. Nero

Pen and brown ink. 5.8 × 4.2 cm

1858-6-26-156

Literature: Van der Gucht, 26; Hind, 78.

This has previously been inaccurately identified as a copy after a coin of Vitellius.

129. Sestertius of Nero

Coin struck at Lyon in AD 66–68. 3.7 cm

British Museum, Department of Coins and Medals

BMC Nero 321

130. Vespasian

Pen and brown ink. 6 × 4.5 cm

1858-6-26-157

Literature: Van der Gucht, 27; Hind, 79.

Most probably copied from a sestertius, such as that exhibited for comparison (see no. 129).

125

126

127

128

130

129

131. Bust of 'Seneca'

Pen and brown ink, with traces of black chalk. Some of the principal lines indented with a stylus. 12.5 × 9.6 cm

Provenance: J. Richardson, senior; J. Richardson, junior; Professor Jansen.

1858-7-24-2

Literature: Hind, 54.

This is a preparatory drawing for an etching which has been attributed in its first state to both Rubens and Van Dyck. This state before letters is known only from the impression in the British Museum (see no. 132). In the second state work on the plate was completed by Lucas Vorsterman with the graver. Although Hind attributed the preliminary etching of the first state to Rubens, it seems to us very possible that Vorsterman himself was responsible for the execution of this print in all its states. Jonathan Richardson, junior, in an inscription on the mount of this drawing, noted a connection between it and the antique sculpture then known as 'Seneca in the Bath' formerly in the Villa Borghese in Rome and now in the Louvre; however, although the features in the etching are similar, in the statue the head is bald on top. This statue was in fact originally intended to represent an African fisherman. True to his inventive urge Rubens has combined in this drawing the upward glance of the fisherman statue with the features of a classical bust, which was thought to represent Seneca until an inscribed bust of the philosopher with differing features was found in 1813. There survive many Roman copies of this bust of 'Pseudo-Seneca', one of which belonged to Rubens.

Attributed to Lucas Vorsterman I (1595–1675)
132. Bust of 'Seneca'

Etching. 13.9 × 11.3 cm

Provenance: The Rev. C. M. Cracherode.

R.1a-310

Literature: Schneevoogt, 140. 42; Rooses, 813; A. M. Hind, *Print Collector's Quarterly*, x, 1923, p.62.

Inscribed in pen and ink by a later hand, probably eighteenth century, *Ex marmore antiquo delineavit A. V. Dyck,* and *Van dijck heeft dit Geést. is raer.*

This is the only known impression of the first state of a print after the drawing by Rubens after the bust of 'Pseudo-Seneca'. For a discussion of this drawing and its relation to this print, see no. 131.

131

132

133. Titus

Pen and brown ink. 5.2 × 3.7 cm

1858-6-26-158.

Literature: Van der Gucht, 28; Hind, 80.

134. Domitian

Pen and brown ink. 6 × 4.1 cm

1858-6-26-159

Literature: Van der Gucht, 29; Hind, 81.

Most probably copied from a sestertius such as that exhibited for comparison (see no.135).

135. Sestertius of Domitian

Coin struck during the reign of his father Vespasian at the Rome mint during Domitian's fourth consulship in AD 76. 3.4 cm

Provenance: Carfrae Collection, 1894.

British Museum, Department of Coins and Medals BMC Vesp. 729

136. Nerva

Pen and brown ink. 7.2 × 5.3 cm

1858-6-26-160

Literature: Van der Gucht, 30; Hind, 82.

Most probably copied from a sestertius such as that exhibited for comparison (see no.137).

134

137. Sestertius of Nerva

Coin struck at Rome in AD 98. 3.4 cm

Provenance: Wigan Collection, 1872

British Museum, Department of Coins and Medals BMC Nerva 119

136

137

138a

138a–e. Five small studies after the Antique

On separate pieces of paper mounted on one sheet.
Provenance: R. Payne Knight bequest, 1824.
Oo.9-20
Literature: Hind, 83-87.

138a. Head of Medusa: two studies in profile

Pen and brown ink. 4.5 × 5 cm
Literature: Rooses, 1403, 1; Hind, 83; H. M. van der Meulen-Schregardus, *Petrvs Pavlvs Rvbens Antiquarivs,* 1975, G.26a, 27a.

These are copies of two Roman sardonyx cameos, both in the Cabinet des Médailles, Paris (159, 160).

138b

138b. Bust of 'Seneca'

Pen and brown ink. 4.6 × 3.8 cm
Literature: Rooses, 1403, 2; Hind, 84; H. M. van der Meulen-Schregardus, *op.cit.,* G.77a.

This could be a much reduced copy after the marble bust of 'Seneca' which Rubens brought back with him from Italy in 1608, after which he did several copies (see nos.117,118,131). It is more probable, however, that it is after a gem of 'Seneca'. One of these we know the artist's son, Albert, sold to the Duke of Buckingham.

138c. Head of Caracalla: profile in oval

Pen and brown ink. 4 × 3 cm
Literature: Rooses 1403, 3; Hind, 85

138c

138d. Head of Minerva

Pen and brown ink. 4.7 × 4 cm
Literature: Rooses, 1403, 4; Hind, 86; H. M. van der Meulen-Schregardus, *op.cit,* G.32a.

It is not certain whether this is copied from a coin or a gem. The crest of Minerva's helmet is missing which indicates that the drawing has been cut down.

138d

138e. Dancing satyr

Pen and brown ink. 5.4 × 3.7 cm
Literature: Rooses, 1403, 5; Hind, 87; H. M. van der Meulen-Schregardus, *op.cit.,* G.38a.

This is a copy of a cameo which belonged to Rubens and was listed in his index of 1628 as 'Bacchus Singing'. The drawing has clearly been cut down as parts of the design are missing.

138e

139

139. Sheet with numerous studies of heads

Pen and brown ink. 19.1 × 14.4 cm

1859-8-6-84

Literature: Hind, 88.

On the *verso* are inscribed lines from a Latin poem
probably in Rubens's own hand which ridicule the
English claim to the French throne.

These studies are evidently based on antique profiles and
are executed in the manner of his copies after antique or
pseudo-antique coins.

190. The martyrdom of St Paul.
71 × 51.5 cm.

195. Trees
reflected in
water at sunset.
27.6 × 45.4 cm.

73. Study for
Mary
Magdalene.
33.5 × 24.3 cm.

191. Landscape with a stream overhung with trees.
20.4 × 30.8 cm.

70. A lioness.
39.6 × 23.5 cm.

154.

61.

158.

37.

140

141

The Jesuit Church

On 20 March 1620, Rubens concluded a contract with the Jesuit College of Antwerp for the decoration of their church, St Carlo Borromeo (formerly St Ignatius). He had already played a part in the construction of the church and painted altarpieces for it. Now he agreed to supply, by the end of the year, thirty-nine ceiling paintings for the aisles and the galleries above, two large canvases depicting the miracles of two Jesuit saints, St Ignatius Loyola and St Francis Xavier, as well as designs for other decorations in various media (e.g. the marble relief on the façade, see nos.140-2). The compositions for the ceiling paintings were sketched by the master himself and executed by the studio, largely by Van Dyck. This was the most important commission Rubens received in his home town, and it was a triumphant success. The artist's friend, Wouverius, wrote, 'The magnificence of the interior of the edifice turns the thoughts to the abode of heaven'. Unfortunately the decorative scheme no longer exists, destroyed for the most part by fire in the eighteenth century. Nevertheless, several artists sketched copies of the designs and these, together with the surviving canvases, preparatory sketches and prints based on the designs (see nos.143-5) give a clear impression of the church's original splendour.

140. An angel blowing a trumpet holding it with both hands

Black chalk, heightened with white chalk, strengthened in part with pen and brown ink, squared in black chalk. 24.5 × 28.3 cm

Provenance: J. Richardson, senior; C. Fairfax Murray. New York, Pierpont Morgan Library, (I.233).

Literature: Glück-Haberditzl, 128; Held, 144.

This and the pendant drawing (no.142) are designs for the two marble high reliefs decorating the spandrels over the central doorway of the west front of the Church of St Carlo Borromeo, Antwerp, built about 1617–20.

141. A cartouche supported by cherubs

Pen and brush and brown ink over an underdrawing in black chalk, heightened with white bodycolour, squared for transfer. 37 × 26.7 cm

Provenance: T. Hudson; R. Payne Knight bequest, 1824. Oo.9-28

Literature: Hind, 41; Held, Add. 172; Burchard-d'Hulst, 117.

Study for the stone relief, probably executed by Colyns de Nole, in the middle of the central bay of the west front of the Jesuit Church of St Ignatius, Antwerp, now St Carlo Borromeo.

Opposite page

37. Ignudo turning towards the right, 38.9 × 27.8 cm

61. Venus lamenting over the dead Adonis. 21.6 × 15.2 cm

154. Portrait of Isabella Brant, the artist's first wife. 38.1 × 29.2 cm

158. Portrait of Sir Theodore Turquet de Mayerne. 31.1 × 21.9 cm

P. P. Rub. delin. & excud.   *CVM PRIVILEGIIS.*   Chriftoffel Iegher fc.

143

142. An angel blowing a trumpet holding it with one hand

Black chalk, heightened with white chalk, strengthened in part with pen and brown ink, squared in black chalk. 25.1 × 27.4 cm. The drawing has been trimmed along the curve of the spandrel.

Provenance: J. Richardson, senior; H. S. Reitlinger; M. B. Asscher; gift of the Fellows of the Pierpont Morgan Library with the special assistance of Walter C. Baker and Mr and Mrs Carl Stern.

New York, Pierpont Morgan Library, (1957. I)

Literature: Held, 145.

For a description of this drawing's function see no. 140.

Christoffel Jegher (1596–c. 1652)
143. The coronation of the Virgin

Woodcut. 34.2 × 44.7 cm

1874-8-8-1362

Literature: Schneevoogt, 79. 40.

This woodcut is derived from the *modello* in the Louvre (KdK 213) and not the ceiling canvas formerly in the Jesuit Church in Antwerp. Both the Virgin's crown and the dove are represented as they are in the Louvre *modello*. One minor difference is that the angels' heads below the

142

144

Virgin's feet have been omitted in the woodcut. This change would have been made clear to Jegher from a design supplied to him by Rubens. Like the *Temptation of Christ* (no.145) this woodcut was first printed in 1633.

144. St Catherine in the clouds

Etching, with some engraving. 30.2 × 20.2 cm
Provenance: J. Sheepshanks.

Sheepshanks 5379

Literature: A. M. Hind, *Print Collector's Quarterly,* x, 1923, p.62; van den Wijngaert, p.88, no.595; J. R. Martin, *Corpus Rubenianum,* i, *The Ceiling Paintings of the Jesuit Church in Antwerp,* 1968, pp.145–7.

This print, here in its second state, before the addition of Rubens's signature, is based, according to Martin, on the *modello* for one of the ceiling paintings formerly in the Jesuit Church in Antwerp, rather than the ceiling painting itself. The oblong format has been changed to an upright one, and the broken wheel on the clouds has replaced the recumbent tyrant, Emperor Maximian.

Opinion is divided about the authorship of the etching, but what is certain is that a counterproof in the Metropolitan Museum, New York, of the first state (otherwise unknown) has been corrected by Rubens in pen and brown ink. Hind's view is that it is the one etching associated with Rubens, which on grounds of quality can be accepted as by him. Wijngaert rejected this proposal attributing the etched work to Pieter Soutman, and the engraving of the second and third states to Lucas Vosterman I.

Christoffel Jegher (1596–*c*.1652)
145. The temptation of Christ

Woodcut. 32.7 × 43.5 cm
1874-8-8-1363
Literature: Schneevoogt, 28.138.

This fine woodcut is based in reverse on the *modello* in the collection of Count Antoine Seilern for one of the cycle of ceiling canvases formerly in the Jesuit Church in Antwerp. The composition has, however, been widened beyond the octagonal shape of the oil-sketch to permit Rubens to elaborate the rock formation and trees behind Christ's back, and to add the pine trees on the right. A charming addition is the squirrel precariously balanced above Christ's head. We know that Rubens supervised the production of this woodcut as an early proof exists, now in the Bibliothèque Nationale, Paris, printed before work on the block was completed, on which he has made corrections in bodycolour and wash. The oil-sketches for the cycle were retained by Rubens in his studio, and would thus have been accessible to his engravers. It is very likely that Rubens would have supplied Jegher with a pen and ink design from which to work. Balthasar Moretus printed the completed woodcut for Rubens on 3 September 1633.

145

146. St Clare of Assisi

Oil on panel. 14.6 × 22 cm

Provenance: ? C. Spruyt; presented by Chambers Hall to Oxford University, 1855.

Oxford, Ashmolean Museum (381)

Literature: P. Buschmann, *Onze Kunst,* xxix, 1916, pp.16–17; Puyvelde, *Esquisses,* p.27; J. R. Martin, *Corpus Rubenianum,* i, *The Ceiling Paintings for the Jesuit Church in Antwerp,* no.39a.

In this initial sketch for a canvas on the ceiling of the Jesuit Church the details of the composition of the final painting are already clearly established. Only in one important particular do they differ. The nun on the right is represented both in this sketch and the *modello* executed in colour, now in a private collection in Paris (J. R. Martin, *op. cit.,* no.39b), standing and bending forward from the waist. In the ceiling painting she is kneeling, a change made, according to Martin, at the insistence of the Jesuit Fathers.

146

147. The flight of St Barbara

Oil on panel. 32 × 45.7 cm

Provenance: J. Sansot; A. and S. de Groot; N. J. Desenfans; Bourgeois bequest, 1811.

Dulwich College Picture Gallery (125)

Literature: J. R. Martin, *Corpus Rubenianum,* i, *The Ceiling Paintings for the Jesuit Church in Antwerp,* 1968, no.31b.

This sketch, which differs only in minor details from the freely executed grisaille in Oxford, was produced by Rubens for the guidance of the assistants who were to work on the ceiling canvas. Rubens has increased the height of the tower and inserted a window in its lower storey. In the ceiling canvas, whose appearance we know from various drawn and engraved sources, the steps were replaced by rising ground, and the pursuing figure of the saint's father is placed lower down.

147

148

148. St Gregory Nazianzus

Black chalk, with traces of white. 41.1 × 47.6 cm
Provenance: Sir T. Lawrence; John Hay; Clarence L. Hay.
Cambridge, Mass., Fogg Art Museum
Literature: Held, 47; J. R. Martin, *Corpus Rubenianum, i,
The Ceiling Paintings for the Jesuit Church in Antwerp,*
1968, no.25a.

This is one of the few surviving drawings connected with
the ceiling paintings of the Jesuit Church. In this beautiful
study the mature Rubens has achieved a fine balance
between sculptural monumentality and baroque exub-
erance. In the equally spirited oil-sketch at Buffalo,
Rubens has simplified the composition by omitting the
large angel on the left, as well as the larger of the two
demons. This may have been done so as not to overcrowd
the octagonal format of the ceiling painting. Held also
makes the plausible suggestion that the devil may have
been left out so that he could be used in the large painting
on the high altar, the *Miracles of St Ignatius.* Such stage-
management would be quite characteristic of Rubens.
Earlier this same devil had featured in the *Fall of the Damned*
at Munich (KdK 194). One should also compare the large
angel he has omitted with the angel in the drawing for an
engraving of the *Flight into Egypt* (no.171) and the figure of
Mercury descending in the drawing in the Victoria and
Albert Museum (no.152).

149. Studies for figures in 'The Miracles of St Francis Xavier'

Black chalk. 35.3 × 53.6 cm (large sheet) and
20.7 × 29.5 cm (small sheet, which has been pasted on the
larger one).
Provenance: Sir B. West; Sir T. Lawrence; Miss
E. F. Dalton.
London, Victoria and Albert Museum (D.904 & 905-
1900)
Literature: Glück-Haberditzl, 121; Burchard-d'Hulst,
114.

Inscribed with the pen by an unknown hand, lower left,
*Rubbens fecit uit't grote autaer stuk van de Paters Jesuite te
Antwerpen van St Ignatius* ('Rubens made this for the high
altarpiece of the Jesuit Fathers of St Ignatius at Antwerp');
and above centre, *P. P. Rubbens.*

The study on the larger sheet is for the figure of the man
raised from the dead in *The Miracles of St Francis Xavier*
(KdK 205), the altarpiece painted for the high altar in St
Carlo Borromeo, formerly the Church of St Ignatius,
Antwerp. It was intended to be exhibited alternately with a
companion painting, *The Miracles of St Ignatius Loyola*
(KdK 204). Both paintings are now in the Kunsthistor-
isches Museum in Vienna.

It is interesting to note that Rubens had earlier used the
same male nude model posed in a very similar position for
the resurrected man in the lower left-hand corner of the
'Great' *Last Judgment* in Munich (KdK 118) of about
1615–16.

Architecture and diplomacy

Facciata del Palazzo del Sig.^r Luigi Centurione Marchese de Morsascho.

IX.

150

In 1622 Rubens published a book about the architecture of Genoa, *I Palazzi di Genova* (the Palaces of Genoa). Unlike the usual architectural publications of the period, this was neither a book of designs for builders nor a theoretical work on the various orders of classical architecture. Instead Rubens was chiefly concerned in presenting to his readers a series of designs of private houses, which had been built in Genoa during the previous three-quarters of a century up to the time of publication. His declared aim was to introduce to the North a new style of architecture, in which the symmetry of classical architecture replaced the barbarism, as he saw it, of the gothic style. In the building of his own town house in Antwerp Rubens gave his fellow citizens a practical example of what he had in mind.

The reasons why Rubens undertook this publication are not, however, all connected with his interest in promoting a new architectural style. Why this book was published when it was, and why Rubens, who was after all an amateur in this field, should have lent his name to such a project may perhaps be partly explained by reference to his work as a diplomat. For it is possible to interpret *I Palazzi di Genova* as a piece of elaborate and courtly political propaganda in support of Spain. An important political event, which affected Spain's vital interests, had occurred in the year before the book's appearance. This was the ending of the truce between the Dutch United Provinces and the Spanish government in April 1621, after which the Southern Netherlands became again involved in Spain's renewed war against the North. To pursue this Spain had to secure her lines of supply for her army between Milan and Flanders. Thus Spain's continued friendship with Genoa was vital.

150. Facciata del palazzo del Signor Luigi Centurione Marchese del Marsascho [Façade of the palace of Signor Luigi Centurione Marchese del Marsascho]

Engraving. 27.3 × 20.2 cm
British Library, Department of Printed Books (54i. 15)
Literature: A. A. Tait, *Palazzi di Genova*, 1968, *passim.*

Of all the designs included in *I Palazzi di Genova*, Antwerp, 1622, that chosen for display probably comes closest in style to the design of Rubens's own house in Antwerp.

A large number of the original drawings for the publication is preserved in a volume in the collection of the Royal Institute of British Architects. Those which are missing from it appear to have been extracted at some stage because of their decorative appeal. Despite the fact that in his introduction to the 'gentle reader' Rubens implies that the drawings are partly his own work, there is nothing in their manner of execution to suggest that he was responsible for any of the surviving drawings; however, he would, no doubt, have supervised the production of the plates.

151

The Médicis Cycle

Early in 1622 Rubens arrived in Paris to discuss the preparation of a most ambitious decorative scheme for the Palais du Luxembourg. Two cycles of paintings were planned, depicting the lives of the assassinated King Henry IV of France and of his widow, the patron, Marie de Médicis. Rubens had attended her marriage by proxy at Florence in 1600. The union was not a happy one, a fact carefully disguised in the paintings. The contract for the series was signed on 22 February 1622 and, with extensive participation by the studio, work progressed rapidly. The cycle on Marie's life was to be executed first, and designs were produced for approval within a few months. In 1623 Rubens went back to Paris bringing nine incomplete canvases with him to finish *in situ*. Two years later he returned there with the rest of the paintings and the cycle was inaugurated on 8 May. The scenes of Henry's life were never completed. Political intrigues in France, master-minded by Richelieu, led to Marie's exile in 1631. Due to continual harassment by the French court, work had progressed little further than a number of superb oil-sketches and was now abandoned.

Surprisingly few preparatory drawings for this vast project survive. The character of those on display, studies for particular figures and details, indicate that the master was entirely responsible for all the designs. Indeed, only Rubens's imagination was sufficiently fertile to enliven the scenes from Marie's most uneventful life. The master also played a substantial part in the actual execution of the paintings, which are now in the Louvre (KdK 243–63).

151. Head of Juno

Black chalk. 11.7 × 11.5 cm
Provenance: acquired on the London Art Market, 1975.
1975-12-6-3

This drawing records an intermediate stage in the preparation of the fourth painting in the Médicis cycle, *Henry IV receiving the portrait of Marie de Médicis* (KdK 246). Here Juno is represented somewhat differently than in the finished work, both in the inclination of the head and details of the features. The *modello* oil-sketch for this subject in Munich makes it clear that the present drawing was done after its execution but before the precise representation of the goddess had been finally settled. The drawings provided by Rubens as models for his assistants to work from in the completion of his paintings are usually larger in scale and closer to the final result than is here the case. The present drawing could, of course, be exceptional in this respect. Its excellent quality makes it likely that it is the work of either Rubens himself or one of his more talented pupils. Of these two possibilities the former seems to us the more likely.

152. Study for Mercury descending

Black and brown chalks, heightened with white chalk.
48 × 39.5 cm
Provenance: P. H. Lankrink; Earl Spencer; The
Rev. A. Dyce.
London, Victoria and Albert Museum (D.517)
Literature: Glück-Haberditzl, 141; Held, 102.

This strikingly beautiful study was first connected by Held
with the figure of Mercury in the *Education of Marie de
Médicis* in the Louvre (KdK 245). The sketch was done at a
stage when Rubens had not determined its precise use. We
may note, for instance, that Mercury has been provided
with three pairs of legs. In the event Rubens reversed the
figure in the finished painting. Such inversions are not
unusual in Rubens's work.

153. Portrait of Marie de Médicis

Black and red chalk, heightened with white.
33.2 × 24.5 cm
Provenance: Padre Sebastiano Resta; John, Lord Somers;
E. F. Dalton.
London, Victoria and Albert Museum (D.106–1900)
Literature: Glück-Haberditzl, 151; Burchard-d'Hulst, 130.

This portrait study of the head of Marie de Médicis was
closely followed by Rubens in the *Majority of Louis XIII*
(KdK 258) in the Médicis series. In the preliminary oil-
sketch in Munich for this painting the features of the Queen
were not defined at all, as precision in such details was only
necessary in the final painting. Rubens made two further
studies of the head of the Queen for use elsewhere in the
series, that in the Albertina, Vienna (Glück-Haberditzl,
150) for the *Prosperous government of Marie de Médicis*
(KdK 257) and that in the Louvre (Glück-Haberditzl, 152)
for the *Conclusion of Peace* (KdK 261). Another in an
English private collection was a model for the head in the
Marriage of Henry IV and Marie de Médicis (KdK 249).

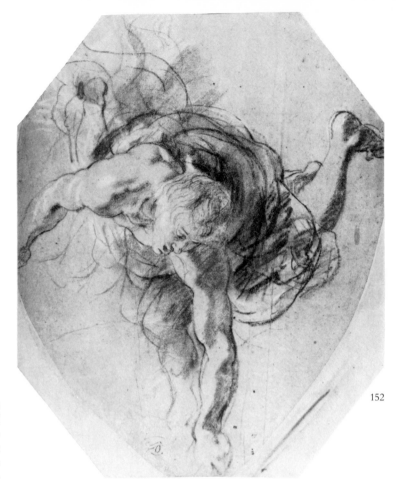

152

153

Portraits

Portraiture was a secondary part of Rubens's activity as a whole, though a major preoccupation during the Italian Period (see nos.9,10,12,29). Van Dyck's renown has overshadowed his work in this *genre,* but Rubens painted several masterful portraits, particularly those of his own family. The same is true of the drawings. Rubens excels in the intimate studies of his two wives and their children (nos.154–6), executed with great warmth, sympathy and understanding towards his sitters. The studies for commissioned portraits, more formal in approach, technically are equally impressive. In each case the heads are brought to a high degree of finish, poised securely on the shoulders which are often conveyed by a few economical lines. The medium, as in the detailed figure studies, is almost invariably chalk, but with red chalk often suggesting the tone of the skin. Our attention is always immediately focussed on the eyes, drawn with exquisite precision and clarity, contrasting with the subtle cross-hatching employed to model the faces. The portrait of the artist's son, Frans (no.156), is an exception in this group, a slighter sketch made in preparation for the painting at Munich in which he posed, naked, on his mother's knee.

154. *Recto:* Portrait of Isabella Brant *(see colour plate page 104)*
Verso: Self-portrait with Hélène Fourment and son

Black, red and white chalk with light washes on light brown paper. The eyes have been strengthened with pen and black ink. 38.1 × 29.5 cm
Provenance: P. H. Lankrink; J. Richardson, senior; Sir J. Thornhill; ? Lord Clive; Earl Spencer; R. S. Holford. 1893-7-31-21
Literature: Hind, 92; Glück-Haberditzl, 160; Held, 103; Burchard-d'Hulst, 135.

This is undoubtedly one of the finest of Rubens's portrait drawings done before the tell-tale signs of the sitter's fatal illness. The puffiness arising from this is noticeable in her face in later portraits. Held's proposed dating of about 1622 seems plausible. The present drawing certainly served as a model for the portrait now at Cleveland, Ohio. The version at the Uffizi, Florence, (KdK 282) was evidently done near the time of Isabella's death in June 1626 and although the pose is close to the drawing, her features now have the marks of her illness upon them. In the portrait in Berlin (KdK 278), not always recognised as a likeness of Isabella, the face has to some extent been idealised, and this could well be grounds for thinking that it was painted posthumously. Van Dyck also had access to the present drawing as he has clearly made use of it in his own portrait of Isabella, which was formerly in the Hermitage, Leningrad, but is now in the National Gallery of Art, Washington D.C. In this she is seen seated before the colonnade of Rubens's town house in Antwerp.

154v

155

156

157

155. Portrait of Hélène Fourment

Black and red chalk, heightened with white; brown ink
in the headdress, on the eyes, mouth and nose; also
by the sitter's ear-rings, and in her hair.
61.2 × 55 cm.

The figure has been cut round in silhouette and backed.
Provenance: Prince Charles de Lorraine; Comte de
Cuypers; Schamp d'Averschoot; R. S. Holford;
G. L. Holford.

Count Antoine Seilern (64)

Literature: G. Waagen, *Treasures of Art in Great Britain,*
ii, 1854, p.204; Glück-Haberditzl, 234; Held, 114; *Flemish
Paintings and Drawings at 56 Princes Gate, London SW7,*
1955, 64; Burchard-d'Hulst, 201.

This portrait drawing is, as the catalogue of the Seilern
Collection points out, an independent work, not a preparatory study for a painting. It is perhaps the most appealing
portrayal of the artist's second wife that has come down to
us. On the basis of the sitter's apparent age it can be dated
about 1635–8.

156. Portrait of Rubens's son Frans

Red and black chalks. 20.1 × 15 cm
Provenance: J. Richardson, senior; T. Hudson; Malcolm.
1895-9-15-1047
Literature: Hind, 95.

This is evidently a study for the painting in Munich, *Hélène
Fourment with Frans* (KdK 346), in which the boy is shown
seated on his mother's knee. Another drawing of him,
wearing the same feathered hat, in a more frontal pose, is in
the collection of the Duke of Sutherland. In Rotterdam
there is also a preparatory study in chalks of Frans, still with
his feathered hat, which Rubens did for the *Portrait of
Hélène Fourment with her children* in the Louvre (KdK 383).

157. Head of a monk

Pen and brown ink, with black and red chalk.
17.8 × 14.9 cm

Provenance: J. Richardson, senior; T. Hudson; C. Rogers;
by descent to his great-nephew, William Cotton, who
presented it to Plymouth, 1853.

Plymouth, City Museum and Art Gallery

Literature: A. E. Popham, *Burlington Magazine,*
civ, 1962, p.69, repr. p.68, fig. 14.

This is a preparatory study for the *Portrait of Domingo a Jesus
Maria Ruzzola* known from a studio copy formerly in the
collection of Dr Auschütz-Kaempfe, Munich, destroyed in
the last war (KdK 19, right). What evidently is an autograph version has been published by M. Jaffé *(Burlington
Magazine,* civ, 1962, pp.389–90) and is in the collection of
Mr and Mrs E. Verdon-Roe. Oldenbourg dates this
portrait of the Spanish Carmelite in the period 1606–8,
when the sitter was in Rome. Jaffé, however, assigns the
original to a later period dating it about 1620. His grounds
for doing this are stylistic and the fact that the sitter visited
Antwerp in that year. Rubens also painted another
Carmelite, the prior, Joannes de la Court (Rooses, 1149),
now in the collection of Lord Plunket.

158. Portrait of Sir Theodore Turquet de Mayerne *(see colour plate page 104)*

The head is executed in oils, and the rest in black chalk with touches of oil on the collar and some wash on the background and on the cloak. 31.1 × 21.9 cm

Provenance: Sir T. Lawrence; S. Woodburn.

1860-6-16-36

Literature: Hind, 94; Burchard-d'Hulst, 171.

The sitter, Sir Theodore de Mayerne (1573–1655), was successively physician to Henry IV of France, James I and Charles I, and lived in England from 1611 until his death. He had considerable interest in the technical aspects of painting, and it was at his request that Edward Northgate undertook his treatise on the art of miniature painting, *Miniatura or the Art of Limning.*

A portrait of Mayerne was included in the inventory of Rubens's effects after his death. The present study was not undertaken, as has been previously suggested, for the portrait in the National Portrait Gallery, which cleaning has revealed to be a copy of the late seventeenth or early eighteenth century. Two types of portraits deriving from the present sketch have come down to us: those with a plain background, faithfully following this drawing and those with the sitter looking straight out of the picture, behind him a statute of Aesculapius and a view of a harbour. It seems the portrait that Mayerne received from Rubens in 1631 was of the latter type, as in his letter to the artist of 25 March that year he mentions the statue and harbour in the background. A studio version of good quality with a plain background, said to be from the collection of the eighteenth-century physician Dr Richard Mead, is now in the North Carolina Museum of Art.

158

159. Head of a girl

Black chalk with brown wash and red chalk, heightened with white. 24 × 20.2 cm

Provenance: T. Verstegh; Sir T. Lawrence; Sir Robert Peel; National Gallery, London; transferred to the British Museum, 1935.

N.G. 853-J

Literature: Glück-Haberditzl, 230; A. E. Popham, *BMQ*, x, 1935, p.15; Held, i, p.13, n. 1; K. T. Parker and J. Mathey, *Antoine Watteau*, i, 1957, under no.282.

The present drawing is probably the closest in quality to a lost portrait drawing conceivably by Rubens himself, rather than an original drawing by an immediate follower. It is certainly the best of the five versions known to us. The other four are in the Edmond de Rothschild collection in the Louvre (Glück-Haberditzl, 231); The Fogg Art Museum, Cambridge, Massachusetts; the Albertina; the last was formerly in the Beets collection in Amsterdam. Both Popham and Burchard accepted the present drawing as an original by Rubens. The Rothschild version is evidently, as Burchard has suggested, a copy made before the present drawing was cut at the bottom. The Fogg drawing is also a copy, although it too has been claimed as an original. Parker and Mathey have attributed the ex-Beets collection drawing to Watteau. The Albertina

159

version is, in fact, a counterproof of this. None of the above versions is good enough, in our view, to be by Rubens himself.

160

The 'Coup de Lance'

The precise circumstances under which Rubens was commissioned to paint a Crucifixion for the high altar of the church of the Recollects at Antwerp are unknown. The altarpiece, one of Rubens's most celebrated compositions, was installed in 1620, possibly at the expense of the artist's friend and patron, Nicolas Rockox, an alderman of Antwerp. Rubens chose to represent the moment, described in John XIX, 31–34, when the dead Christ is pierced in the side by a soldier, and this has given the altarpiece its traditional title. The oil-sketch (no.160) may reflect the master's first intentions, for it differs in several respects from the final painting, now in the Antwerp Museum. This contention receives some support from the provenance, for the sketch was owned by the monastery of the Recollects at Antwerp, and may have been presented to them by the artist for their approval. It may here be compared with the elaborate drawing (no.162), made in preparation for the engraving by Boetius à Bolswert, which closely resembles the altarpiece as executed.

160. The 'Coup de Lance'

Oil on panel. 64.8 × 49.9 cm

Provenance: apparently first recorded in the monastery of the Recollects, Antwerp, 1753; M. Schamp d'Averschoot; G. Blamire; George Mitchell, by whom it was bequeathed to the South Kensington Museum; lent to the National Gallery, 1895.

London, National Gallery (1865).

Literature: for full bibliographical references and a detailed discussion of the problems relating to no.160, see G. Martin, *National Gallery Catalogues: The Flemish School, c.1600–c.1900,* 1970, pp.193–7.

As there are differences between the design of this sketch of about 1619 and the final work, the high altar of the Church of the Recollects, Antwerp, installed in 1620, it is unlikely this was the final *modello* from which Rubens's assistants would have worked. Despite the obvious connection between this sketch and the altarpiece, common sense has not always prevailed about its authorship, as a number of leading authorities have supported the idea that it was executed by Van Dyck. Burchard-d'Hulst has surprisingly seen it as the only known example by Van Dyck of a practice recorded by Bellori of a sketch being done for an engraver. But there is no corroborative evidence, such as a contemporary engraving, to support this.

The possibility that Van Dyck may have had a hand in the execution of the final painting seems most unlikely and is not supported by any clearly discernible visual evidence. Similarly the notion that the present sketch could have been executed by Van Dyck is highly improbable as Rubens would hardly have given work of this kind, connected with such a prestigious commission to anyone in his studio.

It seems most probable that the present painting was an initial sketch submitted for consideration to the Recollects to give them an indication of what he had in mind and as a *modello* for discussion by members of the community. Its early history would seem to lend some support to this idea.

161

Designs for Prints after Paintings

Rubens, perhaps more than any artist before him, realised the advantages of disseminating his work through good quality prints. Reproductive woodcuts and engravings could be circulated widely throughout Europe at comparatively little expense, bringing the master's work to the attention of potential patrons and connoisseurs who might otherwise have been insufficiently acquainted with his work. Soon after his return to Antwerp from Italy he associated himself with the Plantin press (for his activity as a book illustrator see nos.204–222) and brought first-rate engravers into his service, notably Pieter Soutman, see no.42, who worked for Rubens from 1615; Lucas Vorsterman, who collaborated from 1620; Paul Pontius, see nos.165,166 and 169, active from 1624; Boetius à Bolswert, see no.161, and his brother Schelte à Bolswert, see nos.164,167; and the woodcutter Christoffel Jegher, see nos.143,145,173,181.

The elaborate drawings made in preparation for prints after Rubens's paintings give us a close insight into the extent of the master's collaboration with his engravers. Firstly, the rather mechanical initial task of producing a drawing after the painting was generally delegated to an assistant, or perhaps to the engraver. The quality of this preliminary drawing, usually in black chalk, varies, as may be seen by comparing no.171 with nos.172a and b. The master then extensively reworked the sheet, using either washes reinforced with opaque grey and white body-colour (as in nos.162,166,171) or oils. In the process Rubens often transformed a weak drawing into a practically autograph one of superb quality. In many cases (eg. nos.166,172a,172b) important changes were made at this stage to adapt the original composition of the painting to suit the printed medium. The drawing was then returned to the engraver, who impressed the outlines with a stylus to transfer the design on to the plate or woodblock. In a few instances (eg. no.168), Rubens himself produced an oil-sketch after a painting, the same size as the intended print, which was then used as a model by the engraver.

Boetius à Bolswert (*c.*1580–1633)
161. The 'Coup de Lance'

Engraving. 60.5 × 42.8 cm

Provenance: C. Fairfax Murray.

1891-4-14-647

Literature: Schneevoogt, 48.333; Rooses, 296 and Rooses, v, p.156; van den Wijngaert, 30.

In 1620 Rubens painted the picture of the '*Coup de Lance*' for the main altarpiece of the Church of the Recollects (now in the Antwerp Gallery).

A drawing after this picture with some alterations (see no.162) served as the model for Bolswert's engraving. This is an early impression before the addition of the date 1631.

162

162. The 'Coup de Lance'

Black chalk, grey and brown washes and grey bodycolour, with some slight touches of red chalk, heightened with white bodycolour. The outlines indented for transfer. 60.3 × 43.2 cm

Provenance: P. Crozat; Sir T. Lawrence.

NG. 853–G. 1972. U. 790

Literature: Rooses, under 1345; A. E. Popham, *BMQ*, x, 1935, p.13.

This is the design made for the engraving by Boetius à Bolswert (no.161) after the painting in the Antwerp Gallery. The quality of the drawing strongly suggests that it is the work of an assistant, and that only the heightening in bodycolour is by Rubens himself.

163. The miraculous draught of fishes

Pencil, and/or black chalk (indented for transfer), pen and brown ink and oil, on paper mounted on canvas. 54.5/55 × 84.5/85 cm

Provenance: Perhaps Cav. Gizzi; bought by the National Gallery from Cav. Raffaelle Carelli, 1861.

London, National Gallery (680)

Literature: for a detailed discussion see G. Martin, *National Gallery Catalogues: the Flemish School c.1600–c.1900*, 1970, pp.170–4.

The paper support is made up of three sheets. In the centre the figures, fish, net and shells were first drawn in chalk with probably some modelling in thin, grey ink washes. The preliminary wash now can barely be made out in certain areas. The outlines and some detail have been strengthened with pen and brown ink, the sheet was then substantially reworked in oil in varying degrees. This working sketch was made in preparation for the large engraving by Schelte à Bolswert of this subject (no.164).

The composition on its central sheet is based on the central panel of Rubens's triptych in Notre Dame au delà de la Dyle, Malines. It differs in several details, mainly in the figure of Christ from the painting. Rubens decided to enlarge the working drawing by the addition of a sheet either side of the central sheet. According to Martin, the fisherman on the left was executed in pencil. It seems likely, however, that black chalk was used, which has a somewhat shiny appearance due to its being indented for transfer. Rubens elaborated the composition in oil thus integrating the work on all three sheets into a coherent whole.

As early as 1613 the Corporation of Fishmongers, who commissioned the work, had decided to have their altarpiece in the south transept of the church renewed. The wooden frame for the panels was ready by 1615; and on 9 October 1617 the artist met the elders of the Corporation at Malines. They visited the church together to see the altar. They discussed the price for the painting which they fixed at 1600 florins, in a contract drawn up in Antwerp on 5 February 1618. The wooden panels were then dispatched to Rubens and the altarpiece was completed before 11 August 1619.

It seems very likely that Rubens had made this working sketch some time before August 1619. He would have worked after the painting or possibly after a now lost

163

modello, because Schelte à Bolswert's engraving (see no.164) had already been executed before 28 May 1619.

Recent cleaning of this sketch has revealed that the work in oil is clearly by Rubens, and has finally disposed of any suggestion that it could be by Van Dyck, its nineteenth-century attribution. The underdrawing and modelling is not sufficiently visible for one to be able to have a view about its authorship. As Jaffé has indicated, the penwork is also by Rubens. Martin has less convincingly suggested that not only the underdrawing but also the penwork was done by an assistant.

Schelte à Bolswert (*c.*1581–1659)
164. The miraculous draught of fishes

Engraving. 56.5 × 84.9 cm

Provenance: Messrs Smith

1841-8-9-17/18

Literature: Schneevoogt, 28,141; Rooses, 245 and 1344; van den Wijngaert, 39; G. Martin, 'Two working Sketches for Engravings produced by Rubens', in *Burlington Magazine,* cviii, 1966, pp.239 ff; G. Martin, *National Gallery Catalogues: The Flemish School, c.1600–c.1900,* 1970, pp.170 ff.

The composition of this engraving derives from Rubens's triptych in Notre Dame au delà de la Dyle, Malines. Rubens himself made a working sketch for the engraving

164

which differs in several details from the painting (see no.163). Bolswert's engraving is, like the sketch, on three sheets. It had already been made before 28 May 1619, the date of a letter from Rubens to Sir Dudley Carleton at the Hague in which we learn that the engraving had already been received by Carleton.

Paul Pontius (1603–58) after Rubens
165. The descent of the Holy Spirit

Engraving. 59.5 × 41.6 cm (the engraved area)
Provenance: The Rev. C. M. Cracherode.

R.3–90

Literature: Schneevoogt, 60. 438.

The composition is derived from and closely follows in most details Rubens's painting of this subject of 1619, now in the Alte Pinakothek, Munich (KdK 199). See no.166 for the preparatory drawing for this engraving.

166. Descent of the Holy Spirit

Initial drawing in black chalk and brown wash, probably by Paul Pontius, reworked by Rubens with pen and brown ink and grey and white bodycolour, with touches of pinkish red on some flesh areas. 59.1 × 42.2 cm
Provenance: P. Crozat; Sir T. Lawrence; Sir Robert Peel; National Gallery, London; transferred to the British Museum, 1935.

N.G. 853-F. 1972 U.791

Literature: Smith, ii, p.62, no.176; Rooses, 1351; A. E. Popham, *BMQ*, x, 1935, p.13; van den Wijngaert, p.81, under no.521 (as ? by P. Pontius); Burchard-d'Hulst, 139.

This was drawn about 1626 for the engraving by Paul Pontius (no.165) dated 1627. Its composition is derived from Rubens's painting of 1619, now in the Alte Pinakothek, Munich (KdK 199) which had been commissioned by Count Palatine Wolfgang Wilhelm for the Jesuit Church at Neuburg. The underdrawing and work in brown wash appear to be by Pontius. This was then transformed by Rubens, principally with the use of grey and white bodycolour, with here and there some touches with the pen in brown ink. The composition in the drawing has been widened and extended slightly at the bottom. The arched top of the painting has been made rectangular in the drawing. The most vital differences between the painting and the drawing have been effected by Rubens himself. These are the direction of the Virgin's head and the position of the arms of St John; also, in the group of apostles at the back on the right of the picture, one of the heads has been omitted.

165

166

168

167

169

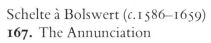

Schelte à Bolswert (c.1586–1659)
167. The Annunciation

Engraving. 43.9 × 33.1 cm

1891-4-14-560

Literature: Schneevoogt, 13. I.

For a discussion of the *modello* for this engraving,
see no.168.

168. The Annunciation

Oil on panel. 44 × 33 cm

Provenance: presented by Chambers Hall to Oxford
University, 1855.

Oxford, Ashmolean Museum (380)

Literature: P. Buschmann, *Onze Kunst,* xxix, 1916, pp.8-
13.

This *modello* was attributed to Rubens by Burchard,
having been previously thought to be a copy by Van Dyck
after Rubens's *Annunciation* in Vienna. It is not, however,
as might seem to be the case at first glance, for the Vienna
painting, executed for the Jesuit Sodality shortly after
Rubens's return to Antwerp from Italy. It is, in fact, for the
engraving by Schelte à Bolswert after the Vienna painting,

and is the same size as the engraving (see no.167). The
Oxford sketch differs in its proportions from the large
painting, being a quarter higher than it is broad, whereas
the painting in Vienna is only about a tenth higher than it is
broad.

Paul Pontius after Jan Lievens
169. Portrait of Daniel Seghers (1590–1661)

Engraving. 23.9 × 20.1 cm (the engraved area)

1931-10-10-1

Literature: Wurzbach, under Pontius, no.122.

This proof, which lacks any engraved background detail,
has been worked on by Pontius in black chalk with light
grey wash, strengthened in a few places with white
bodycolour. It gives us a clear indication of the quality of
Pontius's draughtsmanship in the preparation of his
engravings. It further strongly supports the view that the
first draught in such drawings as *The Descent of the Holy
Spirit* (no.166) was his responsibility and that the subsequent reworking is likely to be by Rubens.

The sitter, a pupil of Jan Brueghel and a member of the
Society of Jesus, specialized in painting flower pictures,
with frequently a cartouche around a subject such as a *Pietà*
or Virgin and Child. Examples of his work in this country
are in the Dulwich College Art Gallery, the Ellesmere-
Sutherland Collection, and in Stonyhurst College, Lan-
cashire.

Marinus Robyn van der Goes (d.1639)

170. The flight into Egypt

Engraving. 37.4 × 45.6 cm

R.3-48

Literature: Schneevoogt, 24.102; Rooses, under 178; van den Wijngaert, 298.

This engraving was made after Rubens's preparatory drawing (no.171). It was twice copied in the workshop of Cornelis Galle II.

171. The Flight into Egypt

Black chalk, with black and grey bodycolour, heightened with white. The principal outlines have been indented with a stylus for transfer. 36.5 × 46.5 cm

Provenance: The Rev. C. M. Cracherode.

Gg.2-234

Literature: Hind, 7; Held, 150; Burchard-d'Hulst, 193.

This belongs to a group of drawings modelled on compositions earlier in date, which the artist has adapted as designs for engravings. The composition is closer in its details to the oil-sketch of about 1625 in the Gulbenkian collection in Lisbon rather than the one in Kassel of about 1614. In the later version the influence of Elsheimer, which inspired the creation of the earlier work, has been lost. Rubens not only greatly admired Elsheimer's own painting of this subject but also had hoped to succeed in acquiring it for himself after the artist's tragically early death.

The present drawing is the preparatory design for the engraving by Marinus van der Goes (see no.170) and the initial work in black chalk has been mechanically done by an assistant. But fortunately Rubens has gone over this so thoroughly in bodycolour that the reworked design is largely his own. It should probably be dated in the late 1630s, as Held has proposed.

172a. The Garden of Love (left half)

Pen and brown ink, grey-green wash over traces of black chalk, touched with blue, green, yellow and white paint. 46.4 × 70.5 cm

172b. The Garden of Love (right half)

Pen and brown ink, brown and green wash, heightened with white bodycolour. 47.6 × 73.2 cm

Provenance: J. Ph. Happart(?) (both sheets); de Thiers (one sheet); P. Crozat (one sheet); P. J. Mariette; J. Gildemeester; H. van Eyl-Sluyter; Earl of Aylesford; Sir J. C. Robinson; Lord Leverhulme; Lady Lever Art Gallery, Port Sunlight.

New York, Metropolitan Museum of Art, (58.96.1 & 58.96.2)

Literature: Held, 152; Burchard-d'Hulst, 180

These two sheets are preparatory designs for Christoffel Jegher's woodcut of the *Garden of Love* (no.173) which was probably produced because of the subject's popularity. The extent of this can be gauged from the number of early

170

171

172a

172b

surviving copies of it. The subject is known to us in three versions by Rubens, and it seems likely that the earliest of these is the painting on panel at Waddesdon Manor, as it was in its original condition before being altered and repainted by him. Burchard established from both visual and x-ray examination that before its modification it appeared as recorded in the fine contemporaneous repetition after Rubens, now in Dresden.

The woodcut by Jegher constitutes the second stage in the evolution of the composition. For it was rearranged so that it could be printed on two halves, which although both made up of self-contained groups of figures could also combine with one another to form a complete composition. Rubens made many adjustments between the preparatory designs that we have and the final printing of the woodcuts. These were all done in order to arrive at a satisfactory solution to the problem of linking the two sheets. It is not likely in our view that this is a technicality that he would have left to Jegher to deal with on his own, although the less good quality of the draughtsmanship on the right-hand strip which was added to the left-hand drawing does perhaps require an explanation; it has on it the ends of the waterjets and the back of the cloak of the young man seated on the balustrade, features which in the print are at the point where the two sheets join. However, the chief change from the Waddesdon first version that Rubens made in the design for the print is in the treatment of the grotto on the right in the left-hand sheet. In the Waddesdon painting the artist had placed before this a large rose tree which obscured the whole area of the grotto. Rubens realised that it would be impossible to represent satisfactorily such a dense dark feature purely in black and white. He therefore discarded it and revealed instead ladies and gentlemen being taken by surprise by hidden jets of water within the grotto.

In the painting in the Prado, by far the most famous version of the subject, the groups of figures have again been rearranged to form an even more compact composition. This cohesion, however, has not been gained without some loss of meaning to some of the details, which one could understand readily in the earlier versions. For instance, the couple on the far left, who in the Waddesdon painting and the woodcut are being pushed by a cupid into joining the other lovers, have already arrived amongst them in the Prado painting, so the exertions of the cupid now seem pointless. Rubens, to arrive at a more intimate arrangement of the lovers in the painting at Madrid has omitted three of the figures from the first version. These are the couple in the right-hand foreground of both the Waddesdon painting and the right-hand drawing for the woodcut and the lady behind them wearing a hat.

Christoffel Jegher (1618–66/8)
173. The Garden of Love

Woodcut. 46.3 × 59.5 cm (left half); 46.3 × 61.1 cm (right half)

R. 4–83

Literature: Schneevoogt, 149. 109; W. Burchard, *Burlington Magazine,* cv, 1963, p.428.

For a discussion of these prints and their relation to the evolution of the subject, the *Garden of Love,* see no.172.

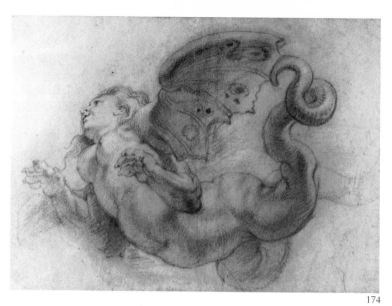

174

The Whitehall Ceiling and the Duke of Buckingham

Rubens's diplomatic career was at its peak when he met Charles I at Greenwich on 6 June 1629. He had come as the envoy of the King of Spain and his aunt, Archduchess Isabella, to begin negotiations for a treaty to end the war between Spain and England, successfully concluded the following December. Charles took the opportunity of inviting Rubens to decorate the ceiling of Inigo Jones's new Banqueting House at Whitehall with scenes commemorating his father, James I (VI of Scotland). Rubens had executed commissions from Englishmen before, notably from Thomas Howard, Earl of Arundel (c.1590–1647) and George Villiers, Duke of Buckingham (1592–1628). The latter Rubens first met in Paris in 1625 while involved in the Médicis cycle, and painted a (now destroyed) portrait of the Duke on horseback. Buckingham may have then commissioned the ceiling for York House, for which no.174 is a study. The project was probably completed before the Duke's assassination in August, 1628. If this was the case, the Duke, the King's favourite, may have shown Charles the ceiling, or a preliminary sketch. Its Venetian flavour would have particularly appealed to the King, and Rubens's confident incorporation of complex allegorical symbols into the design may have prompted him to offer Rubens the Whitehall commission. The ceiling was installed in 1635, and is the only decorative scheme by Rubens still *in situ*. The oil-sketch (no.179), Rubens's first design for the project, may have been executed when he was in England. This preliminary sketch, obviously based on the York House ceiling, was followed by further studies including those in oils in which the individual scenes are more fully realised (eg. no.180).

The rest of this section is devoted to other works and themes occupying Rubens at this period. His collaboration with the sculptor Georg Petel (1601/2–1634, cf. nos.175–7) began in 1627. Petel's ivory (no.176) was, in fact, among several objects purchased from the artist by Buckingham.

Work on the celebrated *Flemish Kermesse* in the Louvre seems to have begun at this period (cf. nos.177–8). Rubens's activity as a diplomat increasingly involved him in political intrigues at the highest level, but, perhaps in despair, he decided to relinquish his diplomatic responsibilities in 1634. His dedication to the cause of peace found repeated expression in the paintings on the theme of *War and Peace* (cf. no.182). The version in the National Gallery was executed by Rubens while in England and presented by him to the King. At the same time the master must have been sketching designs for the Torre de la Parada and other Spanish commissions he had received on his visit to Madrid just prior to his stay in England (see nos.183–4).

174. A harpy

Black chalk, with the background slightly touched here and there around the outline of the monster with yellow chalk. 26.1 × 36.5 cm

Provenance: Lord Glenconner, by whom presented to the British Museum.

1918-10-30-1

Literature: Hind, 20; M. Jaffé, *Studies...presented to A. Blunt,* 1967, p.104; G. Martin, *National Gallery Catalogues: The Flemish School, c.1600–c.1900,* 1970, p.149.

This drawing of a flying monster, half maiden and half serpent, is closely modelled by Rubens on Raphael's representation of Echnidna on the frescoed ceiling of the Sala di Psiche in the Farnesina in Rome, a commission designed by Raphael but executed for the most part by assistants. In the scheme of decoration the monster is associated with cupids carrying the club of Hercules. This is doubtless a reference to the hero's liaison with Echnidna, by whom he had three sons.

Hind associated this drawing with evil spirits cast out in the *Miracle of St Ignatius Loyola* in Vienna (KdK 204). But, in fact, this drawing was used for the harpy in the ceiling canvas, *Minerva and Mercury conducting the Duke of Buckingham to the Temple of Virtue,* a painting destroyed by fire in 1949. The monster is absent from the preliminary oil-sketch for the composition in the National Gallery, London, and was evidently added to the group of animals threatening the Duke at a late stage in the work on the commission, in order to fill what would otherwise have been an uncomfortable *lacuna* in the lower right-hand part of the design.

175

176

175. Triumph of sea-born Venus

Oil on panel. 36.8 × 49.5 cm

Provenance: 1st Duke of Portland.
Welbeck, Notts, Lady Anne Bentinck.

Literature: Waagen, *Art Treasures of Great
Britain,* iv, 1857, p.515; G. Glück, *Vienna Jahrbuch,*
xxv, 1905, pp.73–79; K. Feuchtmayr, in Glück, *Rubens,
Van Dyck und ihr Kreis,* 1933, pp.399–402;
Wildenstein, 1950, no.16.

Rubens produced this monochrome painting as a model
for a cylindrical ivory carving which forms the front of a
salt-cellar, now in the Swedish Royal Collection. The
sculptor responsible for executing Rubens's design was his
friend and occasional collaborator, Georg Petel. It is very
likely that this was not the only sketch produced by
Rubens for Petel's guidance, and no doubt Petel would
have himself made a terracotta model from these before
proceeding to carve the ivory. A drawing in the British
Museum (see no.177), in fact, records one of the alterations
that Rubens made to the design which we find carried out
in the carving. This is the change in the position of the head
of the nereid supporting the garland. Her head is turned the
other way so that she is looking at the triton blowing a
conch shell. Also in the ivory carving the second triton is
omitted. It seems very likely Rubens had Petel make this
salt-cellar for the decoration of his own table, as it was
described in the inventory of the artist's estate in 1640.

There is a variety of evidence to hand to help in
determining the date of the commission of the salt-cellar.
During Rubens's absence in Spain in 1628–30, he left in
charge of his studio Guilliam Panneels, who made a large
number of copies after the paintings, drawings and other
works of art left in his safe keeping. Most of these drawings
are now in the Copenhagen Print Room and amongst
them are three drawings after this ivory carving. From this
we may conclude that the salt-cellar must date from before
the end of August 1628 when Rubens departed for Spain.
This is corroborated by the hallmark which evidently
contains the monogram of the silversmith Jan Herck (?)
and a crowned 'R', giving the date 1627–8.

Georg Petel (1601/2–34)

176. Venus and Cupid

Ivory. 40.2 × 11.3 × 10.2 cm

Provenance: P. P. Rubens; Duke of Buckingham;
J. B. Cachiopin de la Redo; Sir A. du Cros.

Oxford, Ashmolean Museum

Literature: K. Feuchtmayr and A. Schädler, *Georg Petel*, 1973, cat. no. 4.

It seems likely that this carving was made by Petel for
Rubens after his own design, when the sculptor was living
in Rubens's house in Antwerp in 1624. In the following
year, George Villiers, first Duke of Buckingham, visited
Rubens in Antwerp and began to negotiate the purchase of
the artist's large private collection which he acquired for
the considerable sum of 100,000 florins. This ivory and two
other works by Petel, were evidently included in this
transaction, as they are mentioned in the inventory of the
Duke's collection at York House, made in 1635.

   Petel had just returned to Northern Europe from Rome
in 1624, and Rubens was himself at that time particularly
interested in the study and collection of antique sculpture.
This ivory Venus is, in fact, an adaptation of Praxiteles's
famous statue of the Cnidian Aphrodite.

177. *Recto:* Venus with two nereids
Verso: Dance of Italian peasants

Pen and brown ink. 27.6 × 26 cm

Provenance: W. Y. Ottley; C. Fairfax Murray.

1920-10-12-1

Literature: Hind, 25 (as by Van Dyck); Held, 58;
Burchard-d'Hulst, 149.

This is a preparatory drawing produced for the guidance of
Rubens's friend Georg Petel in the execution of a
cylindrical ivory-carving, covering the shaft of a salt-
cellar. Its bowl in the form of a shell, and feet of intertwined
dolphins are executed in silver-gilt. We know that it was
executed subsequent to an oil-sketch in the collection of
Lady Anne Bentinck (no. 175) because of the change in the
direction of the head of the nereid which Petel adopted in
his carving. The dating of this commission about 1627–8
(for the evidence for this, see no. 175) makes it reasonable
also to date the painting of the *Dance of Italian Peasants*
(KdK 407), for which there is a preparatory sketch on the
verso of this sheet, to approximately the same time.

177r

177v

178. *Recto :* Studies for a Kermesse
Verso: Dancing peasants

Pen and brown ink over an underdrawing in black chalk,
with some traces of red chalk. 58.2 × 51.3 cm

Provenance: J. Richardson, senior; ? Sir T. Lawrence;
W. Russell.

1885-5-9-50

Literature: Rooses, 1488; Hind, 33; Glück-Haberditzl,
236-7; Held, 57; Burchard-d'Hulst, 150.

The studies on both *recto* and *verso* are for the *Flemish
Kermesse* in the Louvre (KdK 406) of about 1627 or
somewhat later. One of the couples on the *recto* occurs
slightly adapted in the *Dance of Italian Peasants* (KdK 407) in
the Prado, Madrid.

178r

133

180

179. The Apotheosis of James I

Oil on panel. 95 × 63.2 cm

Glynde, Sussex, Mrs Humphrey Brand

Literature: O. Millar, *Burlington Magazine,*
xcviii, 1956, pp.258–67; J. Held, *Burlington
Magazine,* cxii, 1970, pp.274–81; O. Millar, *The Age of
Charles I,* Tate Gallery, 1972, no.39.

Although the possibility of Rubens assisting in the
decoration of Inigo Jones's Banqueting Hall was en-
tertained by James I and the Prince of Wales as early as 1621,
there was no definite commission or discussion about the
design and iconographic content of the decoration scheme
for the Whitehall ceiling before Rubens's diplomatic visit
to London in 1629. This oil-sketch is almost certainly the
earliest one for the project, and is unique in Rubens's *oeuvre*
in combining a whole scheme comprising several sections
on one panel. It gives us a truly remarkable insight into the
artist's creative processes. How amazingly lively and
inventive the mature Rubens remains in his sketches. He
has lost none of his youthful vigour and theatrical sense
here. All subjects are treated more dramatically and at a
steeper perspective than in the final ceiling.

The central theme is of King James I (VI of Scotland)
who in his person united the two kingdoms of Scotland
and England, being supported by Justice and sustained by

Religion. It is worth noting that the figure of Justice is a
repetition of the nun on the right in the oil-sketch of *St
Clare of Assisi* (no.146), whose pose Rubens had to alter in
the painting for the ceiling decoration of the Jesuit Church.
Victory, or Peace, and Minerva representing Wisdom,
hold a laurel wreath above the King's head. In addition to
the central section, the present sketch includes first ideas for
the oval canvases in the four corners of the ceiling: *Bounty
and Avarice, Reason and Intemperance, Hercules slaying Envy
(or Rebellion)*, and *Wisdom overcoming Ignorance.* At the top
and bottom of the panel are sketches of the two friezes that
link the oval canvases along the longer axis of the ceiling.

According to the normal practice Rubens would have
submitted a more finished rendering of the composition in
a *modello* sent to King Charles I for his approval before
setting in hand the work in the studio on the individual
canvases that would make up the ceiling decoration. Such
an oil-sketch is listed by Abraham Van der Doort's
Catalogue of the Collections of Charles I (edited by Oliver
Millar, in Volume xxxvii, *Walpole Society,* 1960,
p.91 no.77), where it is described as 'the Moddle or first
paterne of the paintinge...sent by Sr Peter Paule Rubin...
to know yor Mats approveing thereof...'. This *modello*
sent to Charles I has evidently not survived; however, there
is a copy of a lost sketch for the central theme in Leningrad
(KdK 332). Original sketches for the two rectangular
paintings at opposite ends of the ceiling (which do not
occur in the present sketch) of the *Union of the Kingdoms*
(KdK 334) and the *Peaceful Reign of King James I* (KdK 335)
are in Leningrad and the Vienna Academy respectively.
For a study of a detail of the former, see no.180.

180. King James I uniting the kingdoms of England and Scotland

Oil on panel. 63.5 × 48.3 cm

Provenance: F. A. E. Bruynincx, Antwerp; R. Cosway;
Colonel T. M. Davies.

England, Private Collection

Literature: Wildenstein, 1950, no.22; O. Millar, *The Age of
Charles I,* Tate Gallery, 1972, no.41.

This finished sketch is a model for a detail of the large
canvas on the Whitehall ceiling. The *modello* for the whole
composition of this canvas is in the Hermitage Museum,
Leningrad (KdK 334). The figure of James on his throne
recalls Paolo Veronese's Ahasuerus on the ceiling of San
Sebastiano in Venice; however, the guardsman is based on
Correggio, and is derived, although reversed, from one of
Rubens's own drawings after Correggio, *Study of a nude
man,* now in the Louvre (Lugt, cat. no.1106).

Christoffel Jegher (1596–1652/3)
181. Hercules and Envy

Woodcut. 60.3 × 35.8 cm

R.4-56

Literature: Van den Wijngaert, no.317

The composition of this print is based on the *modello,* now in the Boston Museum of Fine Arts, for one of the canvases on the ceiling of the Banqueting House, Whitehall, rather than the painting itself. The *putto* who is about to crown Hercules occurs only in the *modello,* and not in the final version. The woodcut is higher and narrower in its proportions than the *modello,* which appears to have prompted various adjustments. Envy's left leg has been placed slightly lower to suggest more space, and the club and the raised arm form a vertical line. This is the only part of the Whitehall ceiling after which Jegher was commissioned by Rubens to make a woodcut.

182. Hercules and Minerva repulsing Mars

Oil on panel. 34.9 × 53.4 cm

Provenance: Mathieu Ignau von Brée; S. C. Tournroe; P. & D. Colnaghi.

London, Edward Speelman & Co.

This sketch, not generally known until exhibited in London in 1963, is very clearly related in almost all details to the brilliant fresh brush drawing in bodycolour in the Louvre (Held, 66, repr. in colour facing p.64). From these two sketches derived Rubens's famous paintings on the theme of War and Peace with which he was much preoccupied throughout his years as a diplomatic agent. In both of his allegorical paintings on this subject, that in the National Gallery, London (KdK 312) and at Munich (KdK 313), the carnage in the foreground of the sketches and the figure of Hercules have given way to the representations of the blessings of peace, fruits of the earth and wedlock. Only in the background are Minerva and Mars locked in strife, very much as in the sketches.

A fragment of another oil-sketch showing only the central figures of the composition is at Rotterdam (Held, i, repr. fig.4).

183. God the Father

Black chalk, with brown wash, heightened with white. The lower corners have been cut and the top rounded. Squared in black chalk for transfer. 41 × 36.8 cm

Provenance: C. Rogers; the Rev. Alexander Dyce.

London, Victoria and Albert Museum (Dyce Bequest 514)

Literature: K. T. Parker, *OMD,* 1929, p.19, plate 22; Held, 170.

Although inscribed *Taddeus Zuccarus,* there are no grounds for thinking that the drawing is based on a composition by Taddeo Zuccaro, nor that it is a drawing by Taddeo or one of his school subsequently reworked by Rubens. The figure of God the Father here is close to that in the great canvas of the *Holy Trinity* at Munich, and the similarly large *God the Father with Christ, and St Paul and St John* at

181

182

Weimar. Held has, however, rightly noted that it is to be particularly associated with the God the Father in the sketch for an *Allegorical Annunciation,* in the Barnes collection at Merion near Philadelphia. Although the raised head in the drawing has been lowered in the oil-sketch and God is holding a sceptre, all other details are so close that there is clearly a connection between the two works. Unfortunately the commission has either not survived or because of its ambitious nature was not executed. Held suggests the sketch may have been done during the artist's stay in Spain in 1628–29, and instances a similarity of theme in the work of a later Spanish master, Claudio Coello's high altar of about 1663 for the Church of San Placido in Madrid.

It is possible that this drawing may have been an alternative sketch by Rubens for the figure of God in the planned Annunciation. But this type of drawing with its abundant use of wash, it must be admitted, would be most unusual for such preliminary work. It is altogether much commoner in those drawings done by pupils which Rubens reworked before they were sent to the engraver. There is, however, nothing to suggest that this was its function.

183

137

184r

184v

184. *Recto:* Studies for the Labours of Hercules
Verso: Two studies for a Visitation

Recto: Red chalk, with one group reinforced in pen and brown ink. *Verso:* Red and black chalk. 30 × 47 cm. The sheet has been somewhat cut down.

Provenance: P. H. Lankrink; J. Richardson, senior.

1897-6-15-12

Literature: Hind, 23; Glück-Haberditzl, 145; Held, 61; Burchard-d'Hulst, 190.

On the *recto* in the upper row there are three sketches of Hercules and Antaeus, and two of Hercules or Atlas carrying the Globe, and between these two groups is a head whose identity is uncertain. Held, by comparing it with a drawing in the Louvre (Lugt cat. no.1228) suggests that it is that of Hercules trying to free himself from the shirt of Nessus. In the lower row there are three sketches of Hercules strangling the Lion, and one of Hercules and Antaeus.

It is interesting to consider the possible sources of the different figures. The Laocoön group no doubt was in Rubens's mind when drawing several of the contending figures of Hercules and Antaeus, as well as one of the sketches of Hercules carrying the Globe, which was also to some extent inspired by the Farnese Hercules. His sketches of Hercules strangling the Nemean Lion reflect the influence of Giulio Romano, and also a woodcut after Raphael by G. Nicolo Vicentino (see no.62).

The studies on this sheet of *Hercules and Antaeus* were the basis for a painting commissioned by the King of Spain in 1639, and completed by Jordaens after the artist's death. It seems most likely that this was the painting of this subject formerly belonging to the Earl of Derby at Knowsley Hall. The *modello* for it is the panel now in Melbourne. Two monochrome oil-sketches are also extant, and those like the ex-Knowsley Hall painting and the Melbourne sketch are both in reverse to the drawing.

The studies for *Hercules or Atlas carrying the Globe* can be connected with the painting executed for the Torre de la Parada, a commission received in 1636. The oil-sketch for this is now in the collection of Count Antoine Seilern. Rubens evidently derived his renderings of Hercules strangling the Nemean Lion from classical prototypes, but his immediate source was renaissance Italian chiaroscuro woodcuts, such as that by Guiseppe Niccolo Vicentino already mentioned, and a woodcut attributed to Boldrini; both have inscriptions giving the design to Raphael. In the woodcut attributed to Boldrini the contenders have been placed in a landscape and this part was inspiration for the powerful and probably much earlier drawing in the Sterling and Francine Clark Institute, Williamstown, Mass. (no.63). Various painted versions of the subject exist, but none of them appear to have been executed by Rubens himself. The outer studies in the lower row on the present sheet are akin to the Williamstown drawing: that in between, however, has more in common with the Hercules and the Lion in the oil-sketch in the collection of Mrs Charles L. Kuhn, Cambridge, Mass.

Although the rendering of the subject on the *verso*, the Visitation, derives ultimately from the left wing of the *Descent from the Cross,* it appears to have been produced after a grisaille for an engraving by Pieter de Jode from about 1630–32. In this oil-sketch the principal figures have been arranged in a compact way, made possible by the widening of the composition. In the present studies the grouping of the figures is changed yet again and Rubens here has considerably heightened the intensity of display of emotion in the greeting of the two Holy Women. We can see no grounds at all for Glück-Haberditzl's rejection of these fine late studies. The studies on both *recto* and *verso* can be connected with particular commissions some time in the period after 1630. Another study in red and black chalk of *Hercules strangling the Nemean Lion,* dependant on the woodcut by Giuseppe Niccolo Vicentino, is in the Print Room at Antwerp, and is datable like the present sheet after 1630.

185. Ceres and two nymphs with a cornucopia

Oil on panel. 30.7 × 23.6 cm

Provenance: Bourgeois bequest, 1811.

Dulwich College Picture Gallery (43)

This is a *modello* for the large painting in the Prado Museum, Madrid in which Frans Snyders collaborated with Rubens by painting the animals and fruit. It has been supposed that the Madrid painting was that listed in the artist's will as *Three nymphs with a horn of plenty,* and that it was acquired by Philip IV following the death of Rubens; however, another version was already in the Spanish Royal collection in 1636 having been ordered from the artist in 1628 but a satyr and a tiger were included in its composition. The differences between the Dulwich sketch and the large version in Madrid are only minor. The goddess Ceres in the sketch is turned now towards the horn which she holds at the top with her right hand. The nymph standing in the background, a figure full of movement in the sketch, becomes in the final version more static with features somewhat reminiscent of Hélène Fourment.

185

PORTICVS CÆSAREO= =AVSTRIACA

186

The Triumphal Entry into Antwerp of the Cardinal-Infante Ferdinand of Austria

On the death of the Infanta Isabella (1 December 1633), Philip IV of Spain chose his brother Ferdinand to succeed her as Governor of the Spanish Netherlands. His arrival in Antwerp on 17 April 1635 was a gala occasion with spectacular fireworks, processions and decorations throughout the city. At short notice Rubens was given the task of designing the temporary decorations, which included triumphal arches, chariots and temples. In a letter to his friend Pieresc he complained that 'the magistrates of this city have laid upon my shoulders the entire burden of this festival'. The variety and splendour of the adornments Rubens devised for the occasion may still be appreciated through his surviving drawings and oil-sketches for the project, and in engravings made to commemorate the event (cf. nos.186-8). Rubens himself was worn out by the preparations and spent the period of celebration at home in bed, ill and exhausted, where Ferdinand came to visit him.

Theodor van Thulden (1606–69)
186. The Portico of the Emperors
Etching. 53.7 × 84.3 cm
Provenance: S. S. Banks.

1884-1-12-47

Literature: Schneevoogt, 225. 16-23; J. R. Martin, *Corpus Rubenianum,* xvi, *The Decorations for the Pompa Introitus Ferdinandi,* 1972, pp.100-31.

The Imperial Austrian Portico (*Porticus Caesareo-Austriaca*) was the most spectacular of all the festive decorations devised at very short notice by Rubens for the Triumphal Entry into Antwerp of the Cardinal-Infante Ferdinand of Austria. This etching is one of the forty-three illustrations by Theodor van Thulden recording Rubens's decorative designs, published under the title *Pompa Introitus honori Serenissimi Principi Ferdinandi Austriaci...,* with an elaborate programme by Jan Caspar Gevaerts (1593–1666), the scholarly city clerk of Antwerp, and intimate friend of Rubens.

The U-shaped gallery of the Imperial portico, through which the triumphal procession passed, was thirty-one metres wide and surmounted by an obelisk twenty-three metres high. On the curved wings on either side of the gateway were twelve over-life-size gilded statues of the Hapsburg emperors and twelve attendant deities symbolising their virtues. The architectural structure was constructed in wood and painted in imitation of marble.

187r

187v

142

188

187. *Recto:* A standing Hapsburg Emperor
Verso: A seated figure, possibly a bishop

Pen and brown ink over black chalk, with traces of heightening in white. 30.2 × 16.7 cm

England, Private Collection

Literature: J. R. Martin, *Corpus Rubenianum*, xvi, *The Decorations for the Pompa Introitus Ferdinandi*, 1972, pp.129-30.

The figure on the *recto* was thought by Burchard to be an early study for the statue of Ferdinand II. This proposal is rejected by Martin who rightly considers the connection too tenuous as neither the costume nor the pose is sufficiently similar. Martin finds the figure of the Archduke Albert on the title-page of the publication *Gelresche Rechten* of 1620 much closer to the drawing on the *recto*.

Similarly, Martin rejects Burchard's linking of the figure on the *verso* with the portrait of the seated Emperor Maximilian I on the Arch of Philip. Martin's alternative suggestion that the figure is not an emperor but an ecclesiastic is more plausible as the figure is holding not an orb and sceptre but the model of a church.

188. The Emperor Maximilian I

Oil on panel. 39 × 18 cm

Provenance: presented by Chambers Hall to Oxford University, 1855.

Oxford, Ashmolean Museum (385)

Literature: P. Buschmann, *Onze Kunst*, xxix, 1916, pp.20-21; J. R. Martin, *Corpus Rubenianum*, xvi, *The Decorations for the Pompa Introitus Ferdinandi*, 1972, pp.121-2. no.27a.

Inscribed above the figure, *Maximilianus primus/No.6*.

Of all the oil-sketches for the statues of emperors on the *Portico of the Emperors* (no.186) this is the only one that has not had a niche added as the background. The other surviving sketches are all in the Hermitage Museum, Leningrad, which also possesses the majority of Rubens's oil-sketches for the various arches for Ferdinand's Triumphal Entry. Two other oil-sketches for emperors were formerly at Aachen, and one, now lost, of Maximilian II was in the Hermitage.

As E. Haverkamp-Begemann has pointed out, the perpendicular red line drawn through the figure was meant to indicate to the sculptor the vertical axis of the statue. Martin has noted that the features of Maximilian are based on Dominicus Custos's engraving published at Augsburg in 1600.

Two Late Works

The two scenes of martyrdom on display (nos.189–90), both from Rubens's last years, indicate that despite his rapidly deteriorating health, his creative powers never lost their strength. They are among his boldest, most impressive and moving compositions. The *Martyrdom of St Andrew* (no.189) may be compared in style and technique with the other drawings made in preparation for prints after the master's paintings (see nos.162–3, 166). The *Martyrdom of St Paul* (no.190) executed largely in oil, is more broadly handled, similar in effect to some of the oil-sketches on panel.

189. The martyrdom of St Andrew

Black chalk with brown wash, heightened with white and strengthened with grey bodycolour, on grey paper.
57.8 × 44.3 cm

Provenance: P. Crozat; La Live de Jully; P. J. Mariette; Randon de Boisset; Vassal de St Hubert; Le Brun; Marquis de Lagoy; Sir T. Lawrence.
1898-3-28-2
Literature: Rooses, 1353; Hind, 13; Held, under 150; H. Vlieghe, *Corpus Rubenianum,* viii, *Saints I,* 1972, p.91, under no.62b.

This is a preparatory drawing for an engraving edited by J. Dierckx, which Hind regarded as a design executed by Rubens himself for the engraver's guidance. Much of the design appears to be drawn by a competent studio hand. It is possible that Rubens may have added a few further touches of bodycolour himself here and there. But if he did, the overall dullness of the work has not been noticeably enlivened. An alternative explanation might be that the drawing was done by Rubens himself but without his usual spirited execution. Such a possibility can never be ruled out in the works of even the greatest masters. This eventuality does, of course, make the task of the connoisseur that much more difficult.

The composition is based, although with some substantial alterations, on the painting in the Real Hospital de Andrés de los Flamencos at Madrid. Most probably painted in 1638, it was bequeathed to the Hospital in April 1639 by Balthasar Moretus's agent in Spain, Jan Van Vucht.

189

190

190. The Martyrdom of St Paul (*see colour plate page 101*)

Brush drawing in oil colours, over an underdrawing in black chalk. The drawing is largely done on pieces of paper on which the artist has made alterations.
71 × 51.5 cm (arched top).

Provenance: ? J. D. Lempereur; the Duc de Tallard; Viscount Hampden; Sir T. Lawrence; S. Woodburn; Sir R. Peel; National Gallery, London; transferred to the B.M. in 1935.

N.G. 853–E. 1973 U.1357

Literature: Rooses, v, p.165; A. E. Popham, *BMQ,* x, 1935, pp.12–13; Burchard-d'Hulst, 195; H. Vlieghe, *Corpus Rubenianum,* viii, *Saints II,* 1973, p.136, no.138a [as by Theodor Boeyermans (1620–78)].

This drawing has gone through three stages of development. In the first it was apparently executed in black and red chalk by an assistant of Rubens, most probably as a record of the oil-sketch, now in a private collection in New York, of the altarpiece now destroyed, formerly in the Convent of Rouge-Clôtre in the Forest of Soignes near Brussels. Evidently the only part of this initial stage now still visible is the three angels in the sky. Rubens then reworked the whole drawing with chalk, body-colour and watercolour. He arrived at the present expanded and more loosely constructed composition by cutting out the main groups of figures and rearranging them so that they are more clearly differentiated from one another. A strip of paper has been added at the foot of the drawing. This operation Rubens carried out with unerring skill, and with reworking in bodycolour produced a much finer and grander conception of the subject.

In its present form the drawing was intended as a *modello* for the painting executed for the high altar of the Dominican Church at Antwerp, which is now in St Magdalen's Church, Aix-en-Provence. The doubts expressed about the attribution of the present drawing to Rubens are misplaced. The most recent proposal, that of Vlieghe, that it is by Theodor Boeyermans (1620–78) stems from the view that the Aix-en-Provence painting is by him, an idea deriving from an eighteenth-century description of the Dominican Church.

A copy of the present drawing is in the Louvre (inv. no.1146).

191

192

Landscapes

Rubens's activity as a painter of pure landscape was apparently limited to uncommissioned works, mostly from his last years, when he was living on his country estate near Malines. But landscape had often played an important part in emphasizing the varying moods of his subject paintings. To achieve this Rubens relied on his own careful observation of nature. In the studies of the countryside and farm life Rubens usually drew directly from the model or scene before him. Black chalk is the most common medium, occasionally strengthened with pen and ink (e.g. nos. 193–4 and 199) or contrasted with coloured chalks to add a more definitive tone to the atmosphere (e.g. no.195). Rubens generally concentrated on particular rural motifs, such as a tree with brambles, a farm wagon or peasants working, building up a stock of sketches to be used at any time. His prodigious visual memory and imagination, however, usually sufficed in the creation of his painted landscapes. Only rarely can the landscape studies be directly related to specific works, though in a few cases (e.g. no.202), a drawn motif appears in more than one painting.

191. Landscape with a stream overhung with trees (*see colour plate page 103*)

Watercolours and bodycolour. 20.4 × 30.8 cm

Provenance: History prior to acquisition at auction in 1859 not known.

1859-8-6-60

Literature: Hind, 110.

Although Van Dyck was a frequent user of bodycolour in his landscape sketches, the attribution of this drawing to Rubens is reasonably certain through a comparison of the style of its execution with his painted landscape oil-sketches. Its colouring and the distinctive use of a reddish brown to emphasise the outline of the bark of the trees should be particularly noted. Unfortunately, however, there is no other similar landscape drawing in the same media on paper on the same scale known to us with which it can be compared.

192. Landscape with farm building at sunset

Oil on panel. 27 × 39 cm

Provenance: Presented by Chambers Hall to Oxford University, 1855.

Oxford, Ashmolean Museum (386)

Literature: KdK 414, lower; Puyvelde, *Esquisses,* plate 91.

This oil-sketch served as a preliminary study for the *Landscape with a shepherd and his flock* in the National Gallery, London, a later work, most probably of about 1638. Although Puyvelde has suggested that it was done after nature, it is very doubtful whether the artist would have painted it on the spot. While it is quite likely that is is based on a particular view in the countryside near the Château de Steen, it was most probably composed in the studio, either from memory or from rough sketches. In the National Gallery painting the pastoral character of the landscape is enhanced by the presence in the foreground of a flock of sheep with a seated shepherd playing a pipe. The composition is also more extended on the left than in the sketch to give a view through the trees to distant country beyond. This has enabled Rubens to depict in it more clearly the reflection of the trees in the water of the dyke. Rubens's interest in an accurate representation of natural phenomena is demonstrated by a chalk drawing in the British Museum (no.195). In this Rubens has made a carefully observed study of the nature of reflection of trees in water at sunset.

193. Four women harvesting

Black, red and white chalk; outlines of the foremost
figure gone over in pen and brown ink. 18.1 × 20.7 cm
Provenance: Paul Sandby; David Laing.
Edinburgh, National Gallery of Scotland (R.N. 1490)
Literature: Held, 59; Burchard-d'Hulst, 154.

For a discussion of these sketches for a harvest scene
see no.194.

194. Eight women harvesting

Black, red, and white chalk; outlines of the foremost
figure gone over in pen and brown ink. 21.6 × 25.7 cm
Provenance: P. H. Lankrink; Paul Sandby; David Laing.
Edinburgh, National Gallery of Scotland (R.N. 1500)
Literature: Held, 60; Burchard-d'Hulst, 153.

This and the accompanying small sheet of studies of
women harvesting (no.193) were probably done after the
life, conceived, it seems likely, for a painting akin to
Rubens's idyllic pastoral landscape of *Peasants returning
from the harvest* in the Palazzo Pitti in Florence (KdK 405). It
may be that he was planning in this to emulate Pieter
Brueghel's paintings of country life, such as his *Harvest
scene* in the Metropolitan Museum of Art, New York. As
similar figures to those on the sheets occur in the background of the landscape in the National Gallery, London
(KdK 404) and the painting in the Palazzo Pitti, already
mentioned, both of which date from the 1630s, it seems
reasonable to date these also after 1630.

195. Trees reflected in water at sunset *(see colour plate page 102)*

Black, red and white chalk. 27.6 × 45.4 cm
Provenance: J. Richardson, senior; The
Rev. C. M. Cracherode bequest.
Gg. 2–229
Literature: Hind, 108; Glück-Haberditzl, 171; Held, 135.

The inscription in Flemish in Rubens's hand has been freely
translated below, either by J. Richardson, senior or his son
as 'thee shadow of a tree is greatter in ye water and more
parfect then ye treess themselves, and darker'. This should
perhaps be best interpreted as follows: 'The reflection of the
trees in the water is darker and clearer in the water than the
trees themselves.'

   This drawing is unique among Rubens's landscape
sketches not only for the delicacy of its execution but also
for the insight it gives us into his interest in the precise
recording of nature. In several of the artist's painted
landscapes we find masterly portrayals of reflections of
trees in water which have the appearance of being
accurately observed after nature.

193

194

196. Landscape with a wattle fence

Black and red chalk. 35.3 × 51.6 cm
Provenance: P. H. Lankrink; J. Richardson, senior;
T. Hudson.
1854-6-28-7
Literature: Hind, 109; Glück-Haberditzl, 211; Held, 136.

This sketch almost certainly dates from the end of the
artist's career when he was living on his country estate, the
Château de Steen, near Malines. A similar delicately
executed sketch of a *Woodland Scene,* evidently done at the
same period, is in the Ashmolean Museum, Oxford.

195

196

197

199

197. A leafless pollard willow

Black chalk. 39.2 × 26.4 cm

Provenance: Fawkener bequest, 1769.

5213-2

Literature: Hind, 81 (as Van Dyck); Held, 134; Burchard-d'Hulst, 106.

Evidently it is a study after nature, done in winter time; however, it cannot be linked with a particular willow in any of Rubens's painted landscapes. The bare trees in *Winter* at Windsor (KdK 238) are no more than generally reminiscent of it. Held's dating of about 1620 seems plausible. The former attribution of the drawing to Van Dyck is due entirely to the early inscription 'Di Vandik' for which, however, there is no stylistic support.

198. Study of a wild cherry tree with brambles and weeds

Black, red, white and yellow chalks. 54.5 × 49.5 cm

Provenance: J. Richardson, senior; J. van Rijmsdijk; Sir T. Lawrence; S. Woodburn; Sir T. Phillipps; T. Fitzroy Fenwick.

London, Count Antoine Seilern (63)

Literature: A. E. Popham, *The Phillipps Fenwick Collection of Drawings*, 1935, p.193, no.2; Held, under 131; *Flemish Paintings and Drawings at 56 Princes Gate London SW7*, 1955, 63.

The various annotations on the drawing in Flemish in the artist's hand refer to the species and colours of the plants. Popham noted the similarity between the plants in this drawing and those present on the right of the painting of the *Château de Steen* in the National Gallery. The Helicampene plant occurs both in this drawing and in the National Gallery painting. As pointed out in the catalogue of the Seilern collection, this does not establish a definite connection between the two.

199. Tree trunk and brambles

Red and black chalk, pen and brown ink, with touches of colour. 35.2 × 29.8 cm

Provenance: N. A. Flinck.

Chatsworth, Devonshire Collection (1008)

Literature: Glück-Haberditzl, 135; Held, under 131.

An inscription in Flemish (according to Held not in Rubens's hand) may be translated as 'Fallen leaves and in some places green grasses peep through'. This drawing, and another of like subject in the collection of Count Antoine Seilern (no.198) have been associated with the *Landscape with a fallen tree* in the Louvre. This latter drawing, however, is a study for a detail in the painting of a *Boar hunt*, in Dresden (KdK 184) which is usually thought to be from the period 1615–20.

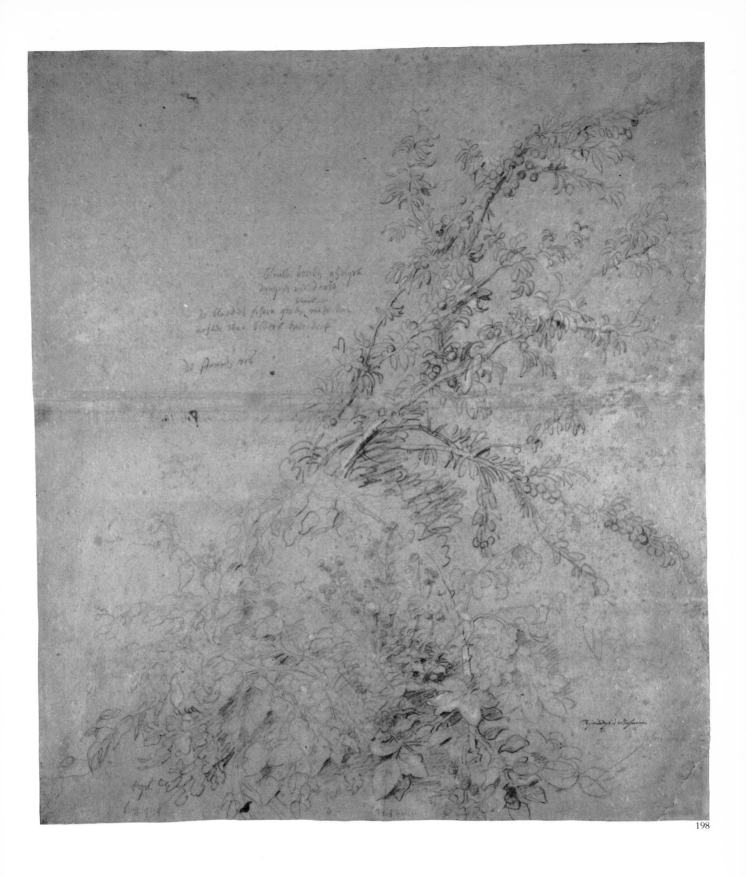

198

200

Sir Anthony Van Dyck (1599–1641)
200. A study of cows

Pen and brown ink and a little brown wash.
31.8 × 51.5 cm
Provenance: N. A. Flinck.

Chatsworth, Devonshire Collection (964)
Literature: Rooses, 1584; A. E. Popham, *Burlington Magazine,* lxxii, 1938, p.20; Held, i, pp.12–13.

The problem of the relative status and attribution of the two principal versions of the study of cows, those at Chatsworth and in the British Museum, has exercised scholars for many years. The British Museum version (no.201) was considered by Glück-Haberditzl to be the original. But Rooses, Popham and others have considered the Chatsworth version the better of the two. Hind thought that both were executed by Rubens. But such literal repetitions do not occur elsewhere amongst Rubens's drawings. Two further versions, obviously inferior, are that in the British Museum (Hind 122), and that formerly in the Northwick collection. They were both copied from the Chatsworth version and it is probable, as Hind suggests, that the second British Museum sheet was drawn by Paul Pontius for the engraving he included in his so-called *Livre à Dessiner.* Of the superior versions that at Chatsworth is more lively in execution than the British Museum drawing. The latter has been taken to be a study for the *Landscape with cows* at Munich (KdK 187) a late work of about 1636–38. But only two of the cows correspond with any in the painting: the one on the left with its head turned away and that sketched in outline seen from the back at upper right. The British

201

Museum drawing is markedly inferior in the rendering of details to the Chatsworth version.

There is some ground for supposing as J. S. Held and J. Byam Shaw have done, that the Chatsworth drawing is by Van Dyck as an early inscription on it states. The use of the drawing subsequently by Rubens in the Munich painting could perhaps be explained by its having been left behind by Van Dyck in his master's studio. The British Museum version does not merit thereby being assigned to Rubens. It is most likely that it was done as an exercise by a talented pupil or associate in Rubens's studio. Popham made the very interesting and probably correct suggestion that Jan Brueghel might have been responsible for the British Museum version.

Attributed to the Studio of Rubens.

201. A study of cows

Pen and brown ink and wash. 34 × 52.2 cm

Provenance: Verstegh; Sir T. Lawrence; William II, King of Holland; Leembruggen; Malcolm.

1895-9-15-1046

Literature: Hind 118; Glück-Haberditzl, 136; Held, pp.12-13.

For a discussion of the relative merits of the different versions of this drawing see no.200.

202. Farm yard, with a farmer threshing and a hay-wagon

Black and red chalk, and light touches of blue, yellow and green. 25.5 × 41.5 cm

Chatsworth, The Devonshire Collection (983)

Literature: Glück-Haberditzl, 94; Held, 129.

As Held has noted, the wagon was used by the artist in three of his paintings; first, in the *Prodigal Son* at Antwerp of about 1618 (KdK 182), and later in *Winter* at Windsor Castle, possibly from 1620-25 (KdK 238), and again in the *Landscape with a country wagon* in Leningrad (KdK 185). On a sheet at Berlin (Held, 133) are chalk studies, with pen and ink, of two wagons. The larger of these was subsequently used by Rubens in the *Return from the harvest* of which there are versions in the Wallace Collection and the Pitti Palace, Florence (KdK 405).

203. Priest preaching to a congregation of peasants

Black chalk, with watercolour washes, brown oil in the upper left-hand corner. Brush in red for many profiles. 42.2 × 57.3 cm

Provenance: Count Nils Barck; Thibaudeau, 1857.

England, Private Collection

Literature: Rooses, 1441.

This important drawing, noted but evidently not seen by Rooses, has remained in obscurity since it was described in the Thibaudeau sale catalogue. There are innumerable *pentimenti,* and the drawing has clearly been executed quickly. The effect of the light streaming in through the open door on the left of the composition has been marvellously captured. There is no evidence that Rubens went on to produce a painting of this subject, although there is a painted copy of the drawing in the Musée Municipal F. Mandet, at Riom, Puy-de-Dôme, France.

The service is not taking place in a church but in some sort of farm building adapted for the purpose. For instance, it is possible to make out a cupboard with a spinning wheel on top, and a ladder leading to a loft. It is quite conceivable that the artist has done this on his own estate and that the congregation may be made up at least in part of his employees at the Château de Steen. Certainly the style of execution of this exceptionally interesting drawing would be consistent with that of the last years of the artist's life.

A fascinating painting by Pieter Angillis (1685-1734), who spent many years in England, based on the present drawing is in a private collection in New York. In this, however, the artist has converted the preacher into a Protestant, and suggested a Dutch setting by the addition of prosperous looking merchants in the foreground.

204

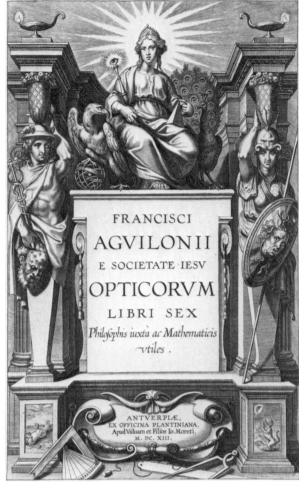

FRANCISCI
AGVILONII
E SOCIETATE IESV
OPTICORVM
LIBRI SEX
Philoſophis iuxtà ac Mathematicis
ⱴtiles.

ANTVERPIÆ,
EX OFFICINA PLANTINIANA,
Apud Viduam et Filios Io. Moreti.
M. DC. XIII.

205

Book Illustrations

As a boy at school, Rubens befriended Balthasar Moretus (1574–1641), a fellow pupil, who in due course took over the important Plantin press at Antwerp founded by his grandfather, Christopher Plantin (c.1515–1589). From about 1612 Rubens regularly designed title-pages, and occasionally illustrations, for the press, one of the first being the title-page to Franciscus Aguilonius's *Opticorum libri . . .* of 1613 (see nos.204–5). The provision of these designs was largely a spare-time activity. Working in close collaboration with Moretus, Rubens apparently had no difficulty in inventing clear and satisfying designs incorporating the prerequisite allegorical figures and motifs with their often complex iconographic connotations. These are usually arranged around a framing device such as an architectural plinth, designed to carry the necessary inscriptions.

Unlike the drawings for his own engravers (see nos.161–173), those for the Plantin press are fresh inventions and consequently entirely autograph. The whole design is often worked out on a single sheet, necessitating the use of several media including washes with opaque bodycolour or even (as in no.213) patches of paper pasted onto the original sheet to obscure corrections made in the process. The finished drawings were copied fairly literally by Moretus's engravers, whose works are competent if not up to the standard of Rubens's own printmakers.

Among the most important designs Rubens made for the Plantin press were those for the *Breviarium Romanum* of 1614, a liturgical book in general use throughout the Roman Catholic Church (see nos.206–10). No doubt Rubens was conscious of the chance offered by its wide circulation of advertising his own capabilities.

204. Design for the title-page to Franciscus Aguilonius, *Opticorum libri sex philosophis juxta ac mathematicis utiles,* Officina Plantiniana, 1613

Pen and brown ink and brown wash. 30.5 × 19.1 cm

Provenance: Sir T. Lawrence.

1861-6-8-148

Literature: Hind, 34; Glück-Haberditzl, 72.

A central pedestal whose face has been left vacant for the title, is flanked by terms of Minerva and Mercury. Seated on the pedestal is a female figure symbolising Optics. In the upper left-hand corner above the cornice, the word 'bases' was added by Rubens to indicate to the engraver Theodore Galle that the lamps should be represented raised on small bases. This instruction, we find, was carried out on the resultant title-page (see no.205).

Theodore Galle (1571–1633)
205. Title-page to Franciscus Aguilonius, *Opticorum libri sex philosophis juxta ac mathematicis utiles,* Officina Plantiniana, 1613

Engraving. 31 × 19.4 cm

1858-4-17-1228

Between 30 March and 22 June 1612 Theodore Galle received seventy-five florins in payment from the Moretus brothers for engraving the illustrations of this book and for the copper plate which is still in the Plantin-Moretus Museum, Antwerp. Rubens received twenty florins for his design. The book is also illustrated by six vignettes engraved by Theodore Galle after designs by Rubens. Aguilon, author of this treatise on Optics, was a member of the Jesuit College in Antwerp.

206. Design for the title-page of the *Breviarium Romanum,* 1614

Pen and brown ink with brown and grey wash heightened with white bodycolour over traces of an underdrawing in black chalk. 34.1 × 22.3 cm

1881-6-11-30

Literature: Hind, 35; Glück-Haberditzl, 67; Held, 140.

Shortly after assuming control of the Plantin press, Balthasar Moretus commissioned Rubens to provide up-to-date illustrations for new editions of the two main liturgical books then in general use throughout the Roman Catholic Church, the *Breviarium Romanum* and the *Missale Romanum.* The present design for the title-page of the first of these has been fairly closely followed in the engraving in reverse by Theodore Galle (see no.207). Moretus ordered this design from Rubens in 1612. The programme, as well as the text of the engraving, were no doubt the result of the closest consultation between the two men. The arrangement of the figures and the text of the inscriptions were provided for the artist by Moretus. Moretus's own rough sketches for this title-page belong to the archives of the Plantin-Moretus Museum at Antwerp. In addition to the present drawing Rubens provided the designs for the sets

206

of plates in this volume. The same plates were in the main used for the *Missale Romanum,* except for the engraving of *David* and the title-page. The latter was replaced by a vignette of the *Last Supper.* Rubens also specially designed for the Missal a *Calvary* and a border design with the *Tree of Jesse.*

Between 1613 and 1616 Rubens received 132 florins for the plates of the Breviary and Missal. Moretus lists in his accounts the ten plates in the Breviary, with the exception of the *Adoration of the Kings,* the addition of a *Calvary* in the Missal, and a *Christ crucified between the thieves.* The latter print does not appear in either book but very probably the design for it is the drawing in the British Museum collection of this subject (see no.208).

207

Theodore Galle (1571–1633)
207. Title-page of the 1628 edition of the
Breviarium Romanum

Engraving. 34.3 × 21.9 cm

1857-3-14-13

In this edition the arms of Pope Paul V have been replaced at the foot of the engraving by those of Urban VIII. Payments for the engravings of the *Breviarium Romanum* and the *Missale Romanum* were made to Theodore Galle between September 1612 and May 1614. A proof impression of this engraving, corrected by Rubens, is in the Bibliothèque Nationale in Paris.

208

208. Christ crucified with the two thieves

Pen and brown ink with brown wash over traces of an under-drawing in black chalk. 29 × 19.5 cm

Provenance: Sir T. Lawrence; G. Leembruggen; Malcolm.

1895-9-15-1050

Literature: Rooses, v, p.64, n.2; Hind 120 (as doubtful); Glück-Haberditzl, 39; Burchard-d'Hulst, 68.

This drawing was among those for which Rubens received payment from the Plantin press between 1613 and 1616 for illustrations, to be engraved by Theodore Galle, for the *Breviarium* and *Missale Romanum* of 1614. It was, however, not used. Hind's reservations about the attribution may perhaps be explained away by the fact that the drawing has suffered somewhat from fading.

209

210

209. The Resurrection

Pen and brown ink with brown and grey wash,
heightened with white bodycolour. 29.8 × 19 cm

Provenance: Tonneman; G. Hoet; Yver; Sir T. Lawrence;
Malcolm.

1895-9-15-1049

Literature: Hind, 36; Glück-Haberditzl, 69.

This is a design in reverse for one of the plates in the
Breviarium Romanum, 1614 (see no.210).

Other designs for this publication are in the Pierpont
Morgan Library, New York.

Cornelis Galle I (1576–1650)

210. The Resurrection

Engraving. 29.6 × 19.4 cm

Provenance: C. Fairfax Murray.

1891-4-14-1128

Literature: Rooses, 1255.

This is one of the plates designed by Rubens for the
Breviarium Romanum, published by the Plantin press in
1614 (see no.209).

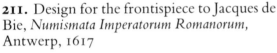

211

212

211. Design for the frontispiece to Jacques de Bie, *Numismata Imperatorum Romanorum,* Antwerp, 1617

Pen and brown ink and grey wash, heightened with a few touches of bodycolour. 31.1 × 20.4 cm

Provenance: P. J. Mariette; Paignon-Dijonval; Vicomte Morel de Vindé; Sir T. Lawrence; S. Woodburn; Henry Vaughan bequest.

1900-8-24-137

Literature: Rooses, 1270; Hind, 37; Glück-Haberditzl 102; Burchard-d'Hulst, 94.

This is a preliminary design for the engraving by Michel Lasne first used for Jacques de Bie, *Numismata Imperatorum Romanorum,* Antwerp, 1617, and three years later in Ludovicus Nonnius, *Commentarius in Nomismata Imp. Ivlii Augusti et Tiberii...,* Antwerp, H. Verdussen, 1620 (see no.212).

The idea of *Roma* enthroned surrounded by bound prisoners and the trophies of war employed here, is derived from a sculpture group which at the beginning of the seventeenth century was in the gardens of Frederigo Cesi's palace in Rome. It was later acquired by Clement XI and is now in the Palazzo dei Conservatori. Except for the attributes, the statue of *Roma* is closely followed by Rubens but the trophies and pedestal have been altered.

Michel Lasne (1590–1667)

212. Frontispiece to Ludovicus Nonnius, *Commentarius in Nomismata Imp. Ivlii Augusti et Tiberii...,* Antwerp, H. Verdussen, 1620.

Engraving. 25.7 × 16.7 cm

1857-3-14-4

Literature: Schneevoogt, 200.48; Rooses, 1270; van den Wijngaert, 3621.

This engraving after a design by Rubens (no.211), had first been made for Jacques de Bie's *Numismata Imperatorum Romanorum,* of 1617.

213

214

213. Portrait of Justus Lipsius (1547–1606)

The portrait in black chalk, strengthened with pen and brown ink; the border in pen and brown ink, over traces of black chalk; a correction inserted on a triangular piece of paper has been made on the right hand of the oval frame. 23.2 × 18.5 cm

Provenance: S. Woodburn.

1891-5-11-31

Literature: Hind, 90; Glück-Haberditzl, 80; Held, 141.

The sitter, Justus Lipsius, was a famous Flemish scholar and leading exponent of a modern stoic philosophy. He attempted to embrace and reconcile the ever increasing divisions in thought and religion in his day. In his search for a solution his restless moves from one sect to another of Christianity are not without considerable significance. Through his brother Philip, who was a pupil of Lipsius, Rubens adopted much of the Stoic outlook, which, in any case, harmonised well with his temperament. He was for moderation in all things, nothing to excess.

This design is for the engraving, in reverse, by Cornelis Galle, included in Lipsius's edition of Seneca's works published by the Plantin press in 1615 (see no.214). Lipsius's edition of the works of the Roman rhetorician, dramatist and philosopher was long to remain the standard one. The influence of Seneca's philosophical thought in the post-classical world reached its peak in Lipsius's own writings.

As with all his other portraits of Lipsius, Rubens based it on that, now lost, of the philosopher by Abraham Janssens.

Cornelis Galle I (1576–1650)
214. Portrait of Justus Lipsius

Engraving. 29 × 18.7 cm

1891-4-14-1001

The design for this illustration to the 1615 edition of Seneca's works by Lipsius published by the Plantin press was provided by Rubens (see no.213). Balthasar Moretus explains in his preface to the book the significance attached to Rubens's elaborate frame to the portrait. On the right the serpent winding round the cornucopia and wreath symbolises Prudence, while the scroll on the other side symbolises Doctrine, and is inscribed with the titles of Lipsius's major works. In the drawing, on the plinth below, Rubens inscribed the sitter's name which in the engraving is changed to Lipsius's motto, *Moribus antiquis*. On a cartouche below again is added in the engraving a curious allusion to the Greek painter, Timanthes, who despairing at being able to portray Agamemnon's emotions adequately at the Sacrifice of Iphigenia, decided to veil his head to get out of the predicament.

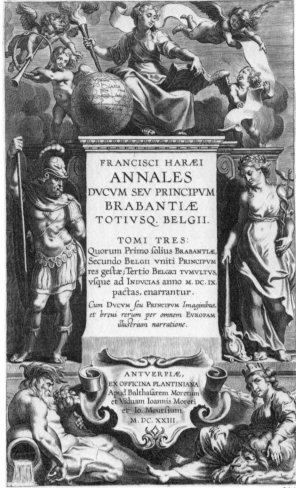

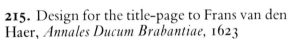

215

216

215. Design for the title-page to Frans van den Haer, *Annales Ducum Brabantiae*, 1623

Pen and brown ink and wash, heightened with white bodycolour. Indented for transfer with a stylus.
28.6 × 17.6 cm

Provenance: Sir T. Lawrence; Sir J. C. Robinson; Malcolm.

1895-9-15-1058

Literature: Hind, 38; Glück-Haberditzl, 155; Held, 146.

Above the central plinth vacant for the title is seated a female figure representing History. To her right a *putto* holds a serpent biting its tail, a symbol of Eternity. Behind him is a *putto* blowing a trumpet of Fame. War and Peace stand on either side of the plinth. As Held has pointed out Peace burning the armour of War occurs later in the *Conclusion of Peace* in the Médicis Cycle (KdK 261) and in the Whitehall Ceiling (KdK 334). Below Peace is seated Belgia with the lion of Belgium, and below War, a river-god, probably intended to symbolise the River Scheldt. This design, executed before 5 April 1622, was engraved in reverse by Cornelis Galle I (see no.216) as the title-page for the first volume of Frans van den Haer, *Annales Ducum Brabantiae*, 1623.

Cornelis Galle I (1576–1650)

216. Title-page of Frans van den Haer, *Annales Ducum Brabantiae,* B. Moretus and J. Meursius, 1623

Engraving. 28.3 × 17.5 cm

1858-4-17-1223

On 5 April 1622 Galle received seventy-five florins for the engraving and the copper-plate which is still in the Plantin Moretus Museum, Antwerp. Rubens was paid twenty florins for supplying the design.

217

218

render was later the subject of Velasquez's famous painting, *Las Lanzas*. The design was commissioned from Rubens by the Plantin press in 1626. For this he was paid twenty florins. An indented drawing in reverse evidently by the engraver is at Dijon.

When the present drawing was recently lifted from its mount it was found it was possible to see through the thin paper Rubens's initial sketch in pen and brown ink, which was obscured by the artist's subsequent elaboration of the design in bodycolour. The adjacent sepia photograph shows this see-through drawing in reverse.

217. Design for the title-page of Hermannus Hugo, *Obsidio Bredana, 1626*

Pen and brown ink, with grey and brown washes, heightened with white bodycolour. 30.8 × 19.5 cm

Provenance: P. J. Mariette; Paignon-Dijonval; Sir T. Lawrence; Sir R. Peel; National Gallery, London; transferred to the British Museum, 1935.

N.G. 853-N

Literature: Rooses, v, p.85; Glück-Haberditzl, 166; A. E. Popham, *BMQ,* x, 1935, p.17.

The supporter, Hercules, on the left of the cartouche, symbolises Work, and Minerva on the right, Vigilance. The crowned female figure below represents the town of Breda, with Hunger gripping her by the throat. This is a direct reference to the siege of Breda, the subject of the book, and the fact that the besieged Dutch were starved into submission by the Spaniards. The moment of sur-

Cornelis Galle I (1576–1650)

218. Title page of Hermannus Hugo, *Obsidio Bredana, 1626*

Engraving. 28.9 × 18.4 cm

1857-3-14-9

Literature: Rooses, 1278.

We know from Moretus's correspondence with the author that Cornelis Galle is the engraver of this title page after a design supplied by Rubens (see no.217), but there is no mention of any payment being received for this in the Galle accounts.

219

220

Rubens and Abraham Diepenbeck (1596–1675)

219. Design for the title-page to Augustinus Torniellus, *Annales Sacri . . .,* Antwerp, 1620

Pen and brown ink with grey and brown washes with traces of an underdrawing in red chalk. Diepenbeck makes additional use of pen and black ink. Indented with a stylus for transfer. 32.4 × 21.3 cm

Provenance: Sir T. Lawrence; Sir Robert Peel; National Gallery, London; transferred to the British Museum, 1935.

N.G. 853-L

Literature: Rooses, v, p.124; A. E. Popham, *BMQ,* x, 1935, p.17.

This is a design in reverse for the title-page engraved by Theodore Galle to Augustinus Torniellus, *Annales Sacri . . .,* Officina Plantiniana, Antwerp, 1620 (see no.220). Rubens received twenty florins from Balthasar Moretus for this drawing. An unrelated drawing by Abraham Diepenbeck of the *Adoration of the Eucharist* has been pasted over the central panel, left vacant for the title. Although lacking Rubens's usual vigour in its execution there seems to be no compelling reason for doubting the attribution of the main design to him.

Theodore Galle (1571–1633)

220. The title-page of Augustinus Torniellius, *Annales sacri,* Antwerp, 1620, volume I

Engraving. 32.8 × 21.5 cm (subject)

British Library, Department of Printed Books (3105 f.10)

For the details of the design for this by Rubens, see no.219.

221. Design for the title-page to the works of Ludovicus Blosius, 1632

Pen and brown ink and wash, heightened with white bodycolour, over an underdrawing of black chalk. 30.6 × 21.2 cm

Provenance: P. J. Mariette; Van Maarseveen; Sir T. Lawrence; Malcolm.

1895-9-15-1042.

Literature: Hind, 39; Glück-Haberditzl, 183; Held, 151.

This preparatory design for the title-page of the collected works of Blosius, published by the Plantin press in 1632, is closely followed by Cornelis Galle in his engraving (no.222). Some of the attributes carried by the angels symbolising the different works of the author are modified in the engraving and Blosius himself is given a beard. Arms are also added to the shields that lie on the dais. Standing on this the four women holding the book symbolise the four monastic virtues. Blosius describes these in the preface of

221

222

the book as mystical contemplation (the veiled woman on
the left), gentleness of bearing (the women with the lamb),
deep humility (the woman looking down next to Blosius)
and mortification of the flesh (the woman holding a whip).

Cornelis Galle I (1576–1650)

222. Title-page to the works of Ludovicus
Blosius, 1632

Engraving. 31.2 × 21.1 cm

1891-4-14-1026

Galle was paid on 12 August 1631 ninety-five florins for
this engraving and the copper-plate, which is still in the
Plantin-Moretus Museum in Antwerp. Rubens received
twenty florins for supplying the design (no.221).

223r

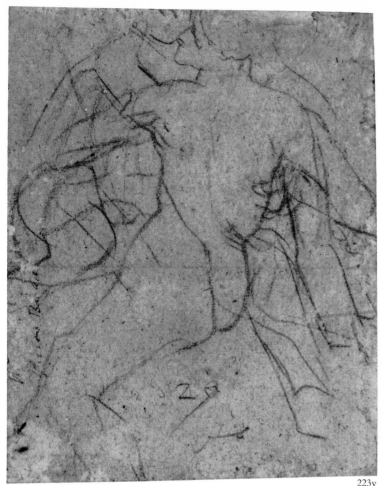

223v

Self-Portraits

These two self-portraits were made for very different reasons. The first, a very personal record, reveals Rubens as he saw himself (no.223); the second, engraved after the painting (KdK frontispiece), for the future Charles I, is his image as he hoped others saw him. In a letter of 10 January 1625, Rubens writes, 'through the English agent resident in Brussels he (the Prince of Wales) has so pressed me for my portrait that I could not refuse it; for though I did not think it fitting to send my own portrait to a prince of his eminence, he finally overcame my modesty'. The degree of informality in this portrait is a measure of the admiration, respect and friendship Rubens aroused among men and women of the highest rank. His gentle manners and social graces allowed him personal access to the nobility and royalty of Europe who, apart from commissioning his paintings, confided in him, certain of his absolute trustworthiness, not only as a diplomat, but as a man. His private life, tragically interrupted by the untimely loss of his first wife, was otherwise as harmonious as it appears in the affectionate portraits of his family (see nos.154–6). This exemplary life did not escape its share of misfortune. Rubens was constantly burdened by the size and number of his commissions, which he was always determined to finish on time. His diplomatic career ended in frustration and disillusion, while towards the end of his life he suffered increasingly from the pains of illness, eventually becoming seriously ill in 1639.

223. *Recto:* Self-portrait
Verso: A man and a woman embracing

Recto: Black chalk, slightly heightened with white chalk; fragments of other sketches in pen and brown ink. *Verso:* Black chalk. 20 × 16 cm

Windsor Castle (6411)

Literature: L. van Puyvelde, *Flemish Drawings . . . at Windsor,* 281; Held, 126.

This self-portrait was most probably done by the artist in the very last years of his life. There are no grounds for associating it, as van Puyvelde has done, with the portrait of the artist in his painting, *Rubens and Hélène Fourment walking in their Garden,* now in Munich (KdK 321). For in this Rubens has flattered himself too much, whereas here he reveals himself to us with an unaccustomed frankness. He intently and seriously ponders his own features without adding any of the gloss of the courtier.

On the *verso* is a very freely sketched drawing of a man embracing a nude woman. The artist has drawn them with their arms in various positions. This previously unknown sketch was recently uncovered when the drawing was remounted.

Paul Pontius, after Rubens

224. Self-portrait of Rubens

Engraving. 32 × 24.9 cm (the engraved area)

Provenance: The Rev. C. M. Cracherode.

R. 4–98

Literature: Schneevoogt, 157.1

Proof, lacking the work on the frame, of Pontius's copy after the *Self-Portrait* at Windsor (KdK frontispiece), signed and dated 1623, painted for the Prince of Wales (later Charles I). It is mentioned in the letter of 10 January 1625 (Magurn, *Letters of Rubens,* pp.101–2, no.60) from Rubens to Valavez.

224

Index of locations

Concordances

British Museum Register Numbers

Register	Catalogue	Register	Catalogue
5211-58	13	1858-6-26-135	99
5212-63	74	1858-6-26-136	101
5213-1	14	1858-6-26-137	100
5213-2	197	1858-6-26-138	102
5237-77	49	1858-6-26-139	103
5237-92, 93	46	1858-6-26-140	104
Gg.2-229	195	1858-6-26-141	105
Gg.2-231	59	1858-6-26-141★	107
Gg.2-234	171	1858-6-26-142	109
N.G.853A-D	90-93	1858-6-26-143	110
N.G.853-E	190	1858-6-26-144	111
N.G.853-F	166	1858-6-26-145	113
N.G.853-G	162	1858-6-26-146	118
N.G.853-J	159	1858-6-26-147	117
N.G.853-K	53	1858-6-26-148	115
N.G.853-L	219	1858-6-26-149	119
N.G.853-M	53	1858-6-26-150	121
N.G.853-N	217	1858-6-26-151	122
N.G.853-O	70	1858-6-26-152	123
Oo.3-9	94	1858-6-26-153	125
Oo.9-18	87	1858-6-26-154	126
Oo.9-19	65	1858-6-26-155	127
Oo.9-20	138a-e	1858-6-26-156	128
Oo.9-21	12	1858-6-26-157	130
Oo.9-23	33	1858-6-26-158	133
Oo.9-24	15	1858-6-26-159	134
Oo.9-26	64	1858-6-26-160	136
Oo.9-27	71	1858-7-24-2	131
Oo.9-28	141	1859-8-6-60	191
Oo.9-30	41	1859-8-6-84	139
Oo.9-31	45	1860-6-16-36	158
Oo.9-35	68	1860-6-16-89	67
Oo.9-54	34	1861-6-8-148	204
1841-12-11-8 (21)	2	1870-8-13-882	37
1841-12-11-8 (24)	4	1870-8-13-883	38
1841-12-11-8 (27)	6	1881-6-11-30	206
1841-12-11-8 (31)	7	1885-5-9-48	81
1841-12-11-8 (37)	8	1885-5-9-50	178
1845-12-8-5	78	1885-5-9-51	89
1846-9-18-5	48	1891-5-11-31	213
1851-2-8-122	50	1893-7-31-19	31
1854-6-28-106	97	1893-7-31-21	154
1854-6-28-107	196	1895-9-15-653	32
1858-6-26-134	98	1895-9-15-828	54a

Register	Catalogue
1895-9-15-1042	221
1895-9-15-1044	22
1895-9-15-1045	21
1895-9-15-1046	201
1895-9-15-1047	156
1895-9-15-1049	209
1895-9-15-1050	208
1895-9-15-1051	85
1895-9-15-1053	54
1895-9-15-1055	16
1895-9-15-1058	215
1895-9-15-1060	30a
1895-9-15-1061	30b
1895-9-15-1064	61
1897-4-10-12	17
1897-6-15-12	184
1898-3-28-2	189
1900-8-24-137	211
1900-8-24-138	72
1910-2-12-192	44
1912-12-14-5	73
1918-10-30-1	174
1919-11-11-22	95
1920-10-12-1	177
1933-4-11-1	76
1935-12-14-4	40
1946-4-13-191	77
1946-7-13-176	80 (Snyders)
1946-7-13-1004	19
1946-7-13-1005	18
1949-5-14-1	9
1949-5-14-2	10
1951-2-8-322	50
1970-9-19-103	20
1972 U.675	36
1972 U.790	162
1972 U.791	166
1972 U.792	53
1973 U.1344	70
1973 U.1357	190
1975-12-6-3	151

A. M. Hind, Catalogue of drawings by
Dutch and Flemish artists preserved in
the Department of Prints and Drawings in the
British Museum, *vol. 2, London, 1923.*

Hind	Catalogue	Hind	Catalogue
1	89	54	131
2	94	55	98
4	16	56	99
6	67	58	100
7	171	57	101
9	64	58	100
10	74	59	102
11	65	60	104
12	87	61	103
13	189	62	105
14 (as by Van Dyck)	30a	63	107
14	59	64	109
15	71	65	110
15 (as by Van Dyck)	30b	66	111
16	73	67	113
20	174	68	118
21	22	69	117
22	72	70	115
23	184	71	119
24	21	72	121
24 (as by Van Dyck)	61	73	122
25 (as by Van Dyck)	177	74	123
26 (as by Van Dyck)	34	75	125
28	44	76	126
29	85	77	127
32	49	78	128
33	178	79	130
34	204	80	133
35	206	81 (as by Van Dyck)	197
36	209	81	134
37	211	82	136
38	215	83–87	138a–e
39	221	88	139
41	141	89	12
44	41	90	213
44 (as by Van Dyck)	78	91	81
45	54	92	154
46	31	94	158
47	32	95	156
49	33	101	15
50	36	108	195
51	13	109	196
52	14	110	191
53	95	117	68

G. Glück and
F. M. Haberditzl, Die
Handzeichnungen von
Peter Paul Rubens,
Berlin, 1928.

Hind	Catalogue	Glück-Haberditzl	Catalogue
118	201	8	22
119 (22)	2	25	38a
119 (25)	4	27	14
119 (28)	6	38	12
119 (32)	7	39	208
119 (38)	8	51	30b
120 (doubtful)	208	52	30a
		56	72
		67	206
		69	209
		72	204
		80	213
		81	98
		82	99
		83	101
		87	64
		91	87
		94	202
		96	57
		97	69
		98	68
		99	70
		102	211
		113	75
		121	149
		128	140
		135	199
		136	201
		141	152
		145	184
		151	153
		155	215
		160	154
		166	217
		171	195
		183	221
		188	58
		211	196
		230	159
		234	155
		236-7	178

J. S. *Held*, Rubens–Selected Drawings,
2 vols, London, 1959

Held	Catalogue	Held	Catalogue
i,fig.4	182	152	172a and b
2	21	158	37
under 7	24	under 158	38
7	25	170	183
22	61	Add. 172	141
23	60		
29	58		
30	59		
33	82		
47	148		
48	72		
under 49	85		
58	177		
57	178		
59	193		
60	194		
61	184		
73	29		
74	26		
82	64		
83	70		
85	69		
86	78		
93	75		
97	87		
102	152		
103	154		
114	155		
126	223		
129	202		
under 131	198		
under 131	199		
134	197		
135	195		
136	196		
140	206		
141	213		
142	67		
144	140		
145	142		
146	215		
150	171		
under 150	189		
151	221		

RITTER LIBRARY
BALDWIN-WALLACE COLLEGE

L. *Burchard and R.-A. d'Hulst*, Rubens Drawings, *2 vols, Brussels, 1963.*

Burchard-d'Hulst	Catalogue
11	34
under 12	19
16	14
18	37
19	38
28	26
34	25
35	24
43	59
50	21
51	58
65	57
66	61
68	208
90	79
94	211
106	197
109	78
110	69
113	67
114	149
117	141
122	84
130	153
135	154
139	166
149	177
150	178
153	194
154	193
161	38a
167	52
171	158
180	172a and b
188	72
190	184
under 192	63
193	171
195	190
201	155